YORK NOTES

Arthur Miller

DEATH
OF A
SALESMAN

Notes by Brian W. Last

BA, M PHIL (LEEDS), PH D (STIRLING)
Formerly Senior Lecturer in English,
Mohammed V University,
Rabat,
Morocco

LONGMAN
YORK PRESS

We are grateful to the following for permission to reproduce copyright material: the author's
agent and Viking Penguin Inc for extracts from 'Death of a Salesman' by Arthur Miller from
Collected Plays by Arthur Miller, published by Secker and Warburg copyright © 1949 by
Arthur Miller © renewed 1977 by Arthur Miller, reprinted by permission of Viking Penguin Inc.

YORK PRESS
Immeuble Esseily, Place Riad Solh, Beirut.

LONGMAN GROUP UK LIMITED
Longman House, Burnt Mill, Harlow,
Essex CM20 2JE, England
Associated companies, branches and representatives
throughout the world

© Librairie du Liban 1980

First published 1980
Twelfth impression 1991

ISBN 0-582-02260-6

Produced by Longman Group (FE) Ltd.
Printed in Hong Kong

Contents

Part 1

Introduction

Life of Miller

Arthur Miller was born in New York City, USA, in 1915, the son of a manufacturer and shop-owner. He left High School in the 1930s but was unable to continue his studies at a university because of the economic depression at that time. By working in a warehouse, he had been able to save enough money to enter the University of Michigan to study journalism for one semester only. Later, by working on a newspaper, and by gaining prizes for playwriting, he was able to complete his studies in that university.

He has been married three times, the second marriage being to Marilyn Monroe, the well-known American film actress. His plays include *All my Sons* (1947), *Death of a Salesman* (1949), *The Crucible* (1953) and *The Price* (1968). He also wrote the script for the film *The Misfits* (1961), in which Marilyn Monroe was the star. *Death of a Salesman* was first produced at the Phoenix Theatre, London, 28 July 1949.

Miller's theatre and Miller's ideas

Miller uses the techniques of the modern theatre to the full. He is not satisfied with simply employing the devices of lights and sound as an addition to the acting, but indicates in the stage directions of his plays precisely when a particular form of lighting or piece of sound is to be used. This is a deliberate attempt to make the theatre as a whole, not merely the actors, express the messages of the play. Mechanical devices assume, then, a symbolic significance—they represent an essential meaning or idea in the play in physical terms. They express a meaning—hence the term 'expressionist' is often used to describe Miller as a dramatist. This particular element in Miller's work will be dealt with more fully in Part 3, Commentary.

Miller was writing for a middle-class audience. His plays were performed on Broadway, the centre of New York's theatrical and cultural life, and in London's West End. Therefore they reached only a small proportion of the population. Miller uses this fact (that the plays reached only a relatively small proportion of the population) to advantage in *Death of a Salesman*, where he examines American middle-class ideas and beliefs. He was able to place before his audience Willy Loman, a man who shared many of their ideals, ones which have been summed up by the phrase 'the American Dream'. The American Dream is a combination of beliefs in the unity of the family, the healthiness of competition in society, the need for success and money, and the view that America is the great land in which free opportunity for all exists. Some of these are connected: America seemed at one stage in history to offer alternatives to the European way of life; she seemed to be the New World, vast, having plenty of land and riches for all of its people, all of whom could share in the wealth of the nation. America was a land of opportunity. This belief is still apparent, even in twentieth-century America, with its large urban population, and Miller uses it in his plays, in order to state something significant about American society. In such a land, where all people have a great deal of opportunity, success should come fairly easily, so an unsuccessful man could feel bitter about his failure, excluded as he was from the success around him. To become successful in the American Dream means to believe in competition, to reach the top as quickly as possible by proving oneself better than others. Success is judged by the amount of wealth which can be acquired by an individual. Success is external and visible, shown in material wealth and encouraged. Money and success mean stability; and stability can be seen in the family unit. The family is a guide-line to success. It also provides emotional stability, and a good family shares its hopes and beliefs. These ideas should always be kept in mind when *Death of a Salesman* is considered.

Another point to consider is Miller's conception of what the theatre should do. He is both a psychological and a social dramatist. As a psychological dramatist he studies character, the motives and reasons behind the behaviour of individuals, and presents them to his audiences so that his individual characters become convincingly alive. Often, these people are ordinary, everyday types, but ones whose actions are made significant by the dramatist. For example, the lives of ordinary citizens going about their daily business in their homes may not obviously appear interesting, but the dramatist can indicate that their daily lives *are* important, that they are interesting or unusual as people and that the audience may see their own situations and psychological states reflected in the characters the dramatist has created. *Death of a Salesman* is a good example of this. Of course, all dramatists and novelists try to make the actions of their characters relevant to other people, and most analyse closely the minds of the characters they have created in order to establish what makes them function as individuals. Where Miller differs from many of the others is in the type of person that he has created. Most of his heroes are ordinary people: they do not seem to be different from anyone who can be met in any street; and this, it might be argued, adds force to his plays, since none of the characters are remote

—we share their feelings, and understand their difficulties. Also, Miller is able to show that everyday people can rise above the ordinary when challenged.

Miller is a social dramatist in the sense that *Death of a Salesman* comments on the nature of society. Miller is concerned about society and the values which it holds. This means that Miller has often been regarded as an ally of the American Left, wishing to challenge the values of society, showing those values as worthless, and suggesting that a change may be necessary. Drama can expose the ills of society, make people aware that there is something wrong with the system. Linked with Miller's attitude to society is his treatment of the middle class in the play. He was writing for the middle class as well as about them. And, at the time he was writing *Death of a Salesman* the ideals and way of life of the middle class in America were declining. People were not as stable financially because of the depression and then the 1939–45 War, and so their way of life seemed to be challenged.

A note on the text

Death of a Salesman was first published in the United States by Viking Press, New York, 1949, and in the United Kingdom by Cresset Press, London, 1949. Miller has made no changes in the play. He has written about this play (and his other plays) in the Introduction to his *Collected Plays*, Viking Press, New York, 1957. The text cited in these Notes is that published by Penguin Books, Harmondsworth, which is easily accessible.

Part 2

Summaries
of DEATH OF A SALESMAN

A general summary

Willy Loman is a salesman: he has two sons, Happy and Biff, and a wife named Linda. He has been a salesman for over thirty years; there is evidence at the beginning of the play that he is tired of his work and that he is not a very successful salesman anyway. He has difficulties with his finances and he is worried about the future of his sons. In particular, he is concerned about Biff, who has not settled down to a regular occupation. Biff is his favourite, and has been so ever since childhood when he was a good and regular football player. Biff's job as a farmhand seems degrading to Willy, who thinks Biff should have 'found himself' at thirty-four years of age. He still dreams of a great future for Biff. Happy and Biff are concerned about Willy, as he has been behaving oddly recently. Biff believes that he should return to city life.

Miller uses 'flashbacks', the recurrence of memories in Willy's mind, to explain the present through events in the past. For example, when Happy and Biff were young, they were content, and loved Willy: Biff was a good sportsman, but in danger of failing a math (American for mathematics) examination, which would spoil his chances of entry into the university. He does, in fact, fail, and refuses to retake the examination. Willy's concern for his sons and his family is connected with the fact that he cannot earn enough money to run his home in the way he would like—he cannot give the boys anything. He wishes he had been adventurous in his youth like his brother Ben, who went to Africa and made a fortune; in Willy's mind he is a model for Happy and Biff to copy. Biff, however, comes to realise that he cannot do this, and consequently is continually angry with Willy for trying to push him into success. He does, however, agree to go and see Bill Oliver, a man for whom he used to work, to try to get a job. This is after Linda has revealed that Willy has been contemplating killing himself by gas.

The interview for this job never takes place, despite the family's hopes, and the celebration in the restaurant is a failure. Happy and Biff cannot tell the real news to their father, especially as Willy himself has just lost his job. Willy dreams of what might have been if he had gone to Alaska, as Ben had apparently once suggested, but tries to draw some consolation from Biff's 'interview' which he believes took place. In vain Biff tries to make him see that he probably will not get the job.

Willy has had an affair with a woman in the past, which explains Biff's changed attitude to his work, and to Willy, whom he sees as false; in his words he sees his father as 'a fake'. In his anger, he tells Willy exactly how he feels about the Loman family's fake existence, revealing at the same time that he knows his father has been contemplating suicide. He does not know, however, that Willy is determined to kill himself in order to let Biff have his life assurance. He crashes the car, and dies, leaving his wife and sons talking over his grave.

Detailed summaries

In this and the following sections, page numbers in the text are referred to: the edition used throughout is the one published by Penguin Books (1961).

Act one

At the opening of the play, Willy is seen returning from work: he is a salesman and has to travel around selling his firm's goods. In fact, he is home early from work and Linda worries that something has happened to him. Willy assures her that he is all right, but that he did have some trouble with the car; not mechanical trouble as such, but something seemed to happen to him on the journey. Linda tries to calm him, saying that he is merely over-tired. Willy reveals that he has been daydreaming:

> WILLY: I was driving alone, you understand? And I was fine. I was even observing the scenery. You can imagine, me looking at scenery, on the road every week of my life. But its so beautiful up there, Linda, the trees are so thick, and the sun is warm. I opened the windshield and just let the warm air breathe all over me. And all of a sudden I'm going off the road: I'm tellin' ya, I absolutely forget I was driving. If I'd've gone the other way over the white line I might've killed somebody. So I went on again—and five minutes later I'm dreamin' again.
> (p.9)

He is worried that his lack of concentration may lead to a fatal accident.

Linda wants Willy to transfer his job to New York, but Willy is determined to stay in New England, the area he has been working in for many years.

Linda realises that Willy is too old: 'You're sixty years old. They can't expect you to keep travelling every week' (p.10). Willy reveals that he believes in his own worth: he could have been in charge if things had gone his way.

Willy asks about his sons Happy and Biff who have been out on dates and are now asleep. He has angered Biff about money, since he feels Biff should be earning much more than he actually is. Biff has been upset by the criticism. Willy does not like Biff working as a farm-hand, an occupation which he sees as degrading:

> How can he find himself on a farm? Is that a life? A farmhand? In the beginning, when he was young, I thought, well, a young man, it's good for him to tramp around, take a lot of different jobs. But it's more than ten years now and he has yet to make thirty-five dollars a week! (p.11)

Willy is angered by Biff who still does not know what he wants to do at the age of thirty-four. Linda is more sympathetic, saying that Biff is lost, but Willy rejects this: America is the greatest country in the world, so a man should not get lost. He could, according to Willy, become a good salesman, because, in Willy's eyes, he has all the qualities for success. He had been popular in school and has the right sort of personality. Willy now dreams of life in the past with open air and trees and plenty of room in contrast to the city life which they now lead:

> The street is lined with cars. There's not a breath of fresh air in the neighbourhood. The grass don't grow any more, you can't raise a carrot in the backyard. They should've had a law against apartment houses. Remember those two beautiful elm trees out there? When I and Biff hung the swing between them? (p.12)

He is angered by this more than he is by Biff and he soon reveals his true affection for his son, thinking he should allow Biff after all to make up his own mind. He has confidence in him, revealing that he would 'put his money' on Biff; in other words, he believes that Biff will be successful some day. He remembers the happy days of Biff's youth, and the joy he used to gain from simple things, such as seeing Biff polishing the car. Willy now goes to rest.

The scene moves to the bedroom of Happy and Biff. They are discussing the situation between them. Both are concerned about the possibility that Willy may smash the car: Happy says that he has been driving very erratically lately, and has noticed some oddities:

> HAPPY: He just doesn't keep his mind on it. I drove into the city with him last week.
> He stops at a green light and then it turns red and he goes. (p.14)

As the play progresses, we observe the decline in Willy's mental state.

The subject now changes as the two discuss their past girl friends, but Happy also uses this as an excuse to ask about Biff's 'confidence' as he puts it, by which he means Biff's former self-confidence. Biff says that he believes Willy mocks him all the time. Happy points out to Biff that he has noticed Willy worrying over Biff and the fact that he has not yet settled to any occupation. Biff agrees with this to some extent saying that he is not sure of what he wants. He sometimes wants success in the city, and sometimes doesn't:

> To get on that subway on the hot mornings in summer. To devote your whole life to keeping stock, or making phone calls, or selling or buying. To suffer fifty weeks of the year for the sake of a two-week vacation, when all you really desire is to be outdoors, with your shirt off. And always to have to get ahead of the next fella. And still— that's how you build a future. (p.16)

He is also confused in that he likes farming, yet sometimes he feels he doesn't:

> And whenever spring comes to where I am, I suddenly get the feeling, my God, I'm not getting anywhere. What the hell am I doing, playing around with horses, twenty-eight dollars a week! I'm thirty-four years old, I oughta be making my future. (pp.16–17)

Whereas Biff feels that he is wasting his life, Happy seems quite different. He could be a success, but he is lonely, even though he seems to have everything. He is attracted by Biff's suggestion that they should go 'out West', into the country, and work on a farm, but he has to admit that he wants to join others in management: he is proud, believing in himself and believing that he can make it too:

> I got to show some of those pompous self-important executives over there that Hap Loman can make the grade. I want to walk into a store the way he walks in. Then I'll go with you, Biff. We'll be together yet, I swear. (p.18)

The conversation moves back to the girl friends; Happy is content to chase women, and pleased that he can take out someone already engaged, particularly if the fiancé is a person above him on the success ladder. He does this in the same way in which he takes bribes: he cannot explain his motives:

> I don't know what gets into me, may be I just have an over-developed sense of competition or something, but I went and ruined her, and furthermore I can't get rid of her. And he's the third executive I've done that to . . . Like I'm not supposed to take bribes. Manufacturers offer me a hundred dollar bill now and then to throw an order their way. You know how honest I am, but it's like this girl, see. (p.19)

Biff changes the subject: he has an idea of seeing Bill Oliver, an old friend who apparently once promised Biff help. Biff needs money to buy a ranch, but he appears to have been sacked from his job with Oliver formerly, for stealing. Willy's voice from below is heard: it is plain from his remarks that he is still thinking in the past, for he is asking Biff is he is 'gonna wash his engine' and tells him 'Don't get your sweater dirty Biff'. This angers Biff, especially as he knows that his mother can hear Willy.

The scene moves back to Willy; he is imagining scenes from the past (and remains in this state of mind up to page 31). He is warning Biff against involvement with girls, while he is pleased with Biff's work on the car:

> Just wanna be careful with those girls, Biff, that's all. Don't make any promises. No promises of any kind. Because a girl, y'know, they always believe what you tell 'em, and you're very young . . .
>
> I been wondering why you polish the car so careful. Ha! Don't leave the hubcaps, boys. Get the chamois to the hubcaps. Happy, use a newspaper on the windows, it's the easiest thing. Show him how to do it Biff. (p.21)

He thinks of the country life and the open air. This leads to the entry of Young Biff and Young Happy. While this is still part of Willy's imagination at this point, the characters are bought out on stage to show what the Loman family used to be like. Willy remembers how he used to return from a business trip with presents for the boys, especially sporting gifts. He encouraged Biff in his football practice. Both boys reveal that they have missed Willy, while he promises them that one day he will have his own business and be 'bigger than Uncle Charley' (p.23), since Charley is 'not liked'. He tells the boys about his trip to Providence, a town in the north, and Waterbury and Boston, towns in the East. He says he will take the boys with him as he is known and respected throughout his area:

> I'll show you the towns. America is full of beautiful towns and fine, upstanding people. And they know me, boys, they know me up and down New England. The finest people. And when I bring you fellas up, there'll be open sesame for all of us, 'cause one thing boys: I have friends. (p.24)

Biff is in a football game; Willy is very involved with this, and urges Biff on. Biff promises that this game is for Willy.

Bernard enters; he is seen by the Lomans as a figure of fun since he is a studious type. Bernard is worried that Biff may 'flunk' (fail) his math examination. He warns him that he has heard 'that if you don't start studyin' math he's gonna flunk you, and you won't graduate' (p.25). Biff and Willy seem unconcerned about this, and Bernard is dismissed .

as an 'anaemic'. Willy does not believe that Biff could fail. Although Bernard is good in school, Willy thinks he will be a failure in life because of his small physique and his lack of 'personal interest':

> Bernard can get the best marks in school, y'understand, you are going to be five times ahead of him. That's why I thank Almighty God you're both built like Adonises. Because a man who makes an appearance in the business world, the man who creates personal interest, is the man who gets ahead. (p.25)

Linda now enters, and greets Willy; the children leave. She asks about Willy's sales and he exaggerates the amount at first, afterwards telling the truth. Linda works out the wages he has earned, and it comes to seventy dollars, apparently a good wage. The house finances have to be worked out. Money is owed on the refrigerator, the washing machine and the vacuum cleaner. There are also some house repairs. Altogether, a hundred and twenty dollars are owed.

Willy becomes depressed about business and reveals that people don't seem to 'take' to him, that they don't notice him or even laugh at him. Linda assures him of her admiration. At this point the laughter of a woman is heard: she is 'present' on stage, but unseen by the other characters; again, she is a voice from the past in Willy's mind. She is the woman whom we see later in the play, again in a crucial scene from Willy's past. As Miller informs us in a stage direction, the action continues through her presence: 'he talks through the WOMAN's subsiding laughter'(p.29). It is a mocking laughter.

Willy goes on to explain his feelings of loneliness and his love for Linda; he worries about providing for his family. Willy's conversation blends into one with the Woman, who in turn assures Willy of her admiration for him. There has been some close relationship with this Woman in the past:

WILLY: . . . Will you come up again?
THE WOMAN: Sure thing. You do make me laugh. It's good for me. (*She squeezes his arm, kisses him*). And I think you're a wonderful man.
WILLY: You picked me, heh?
THE WOMAN: Sure. Because you're so sweet. And such a kidder.
WILLY: Well I'll see you the next time I'm in Boston.
THE WOMAN: I'll put you right through to the buyers. (p.30)

It is obvious that he has a lot of fun with her, and promises to keep up the relationship. Her laughter then blends with Linda's, as though the Woman has been part of Willy's conscience at that time in the past.

Bernard re-appears to remind Willy that Biff could fail his exam, and Willy suggests that he should help Biff in the exam (by cheating), but

Bernard is afraid, as this is a really important exam. It is suggested also that this cheating has taken place before. Linda also criticises Biff ('He's too rough with the girls, Willy. All the mothers are afraid of him!'), and Willy becomes angry. Mixed with this discussion is the return of the Woman's laughter, as though she were mocking Willy. Willy refuses to listen to these criticisms, insisting he wants a boy of spirit. 'There's nothing a matter with him,' he argues, 'You want him to be a worm like Bernard? He's got spirit, personality . . .'

The scene now returns to the present. Willy reveals to Happy that he is scared by his own driving, but he is rambling, and his speech turns to a story of a successful entrepreneur. Happy shows envy and interest, and promises Willy that one day 'he will retire him for life', by which he means he will earn sufficient money for Willy and himself to live on, so that Willy can retire from work. Willy points out that his dreams are misconceived:

> You'll retire me for life on seventy goddam dollars a week? And your women and your car and your apartment, and you'll retire me for life! Christ's sake, I couldn't get past Yonkers today! Where are you guys, where are you? (p.32)

This is a combination of Willy's view of Happy and his own ramblings.

Charley enters; Happy leaves the two together, and they play cards. Charley seems to want to offer Willy a job, but Willy becomes insulted. He then reveals his concern over Biff, and the fact that he feels he should 'give' him something. 'I got nothing to give him, Charley, I'm clean', (meaning 'clean broke') he says in desperation.

Willy's pride becomes hurt by Charley: Willy feels that he is a 'man', good with his hands, and generally superior to Charley. Uncle Ben, Willy's brother, now enters, but it is clear that this is only in Willy's mind, judging from Charley's reaction: Ben has been dead for several weeks. Willy carries on an imaginary conversation with him, and speaks to Charley at the same time, much to Charley's confusion:

BEN: I must take a train, William. There are several properties
          I'm looking at in Alaska.
WILLY: Sure, sure! If I'd gone with him to Alaska that time, every-
          thing would've been totally different.
CHARLEY: Go on, you'd freeze to death up there.
WILLY: What're you talking about?
BEN: Opportunity is tremendous in Alaska, William. Surprised
          you're not up there.
WILLY: Sure, tremendous.
CHARLEY: Heh?
WILLY: That was the only man I ever met who knew the answers.
CHARLEY: Who?

BEN: How are you all?
WILLY: (*taking a pot, smiling*): Fine, fine.
CHARLEY: Pretty sharp tonight.
BEN: Is Mother living with you?
WILLY: No, she died a long time ago.
CHARLEY: Who?   (p.35)

Willy seems to assume that Charley is in the conversation since he speaks to him at the same time. He quickly becomes annoyed over the cards, a sign of his irritable state. Charley leaves, finally annoyed over Willy's attitude. Linda now 'enters': again, in Willy's mind. Willy reminisces over his boyhood days and asks Ben about his various adventures. Ben tells him that he went to Africa to work in diamond mines. Willy calls in the boys, and they appear once more as Young Biff and Young Happy. Willy asks them of their uncle's success, as Willy wants the same thing for them. He wants them to be proud of their background, too. 'Please tell about Dad,' he asks him, 'I want my boys to hear. I want them to know the kind of stock they spring from.' (p.37–8)

Clearly, Ben is seen as a man of action and strength—and he is rich. His advice to Biff, 'never fight fair' (p.38), is the opposite of Willy's attitude. It is also clear that Ben is not very impressed with Willy's occupation, but Willy tries to convince him that life is fine:

WILLY: No, Ben, I don't want you to think . . . (*He takes Ben's arm to show him*). It's Brooklyn, I know, but we hunt too.
BEN: Really now.
WILLY: Oh, sure, there's snakes and rabbits and—that's why I moved out here. Why, Biff can fell any one of those trees in no time! (p.39)

Charley now re-enters. Ben and Willy make fun of him, recalling the earlier attitude of Willy and Biff to Bernard. Willy contrasts the characters of Biff and Bernard: the former is a 'man' and daring; the other boy is timid.

Willy reveals to Ben that he is worried about himself and whether he is bringing up his boys properly, and Ben assures him they are 'first-rate', exactly the comment that Willy wanted to hear. He reminds them all once again of his success:

'William, when I walked into the jungle, I was seventeen. When I walked out I was twenty-one. And, by God, I was rich!' (p.40–1)

Ben leaves, having confirmed Willy's view that his boys should be like him.

As Linda enters, the scene is brought back to the present. Her comment that Willy has pawned the watch that Ben gave him brings the action back down to reality. Willy is lost in admiration for Ben. Biff enters, angry and concerned, insisting that his mother tell him how long Willy has been 'like this' and why he hadn't been informed. This is simply because Biff has had no address for three months.

Linda tries to explain to Biff Willy's state of mind, how excited he becomes when he knows Biff is to come home, but she cannot understand why the two are so 'hateful' to each other: they seem to argue all the time. Linda is upset by Biff's apparent neglect, since she loves him and hates the idea of Willy being made to feel 'low'. Biff is less than convinced by her, and thinks Willy is 'crazy'. Linda insists that Willy is owed respect, since he is their father and he has worked hard for them. He is also owed 'attention'. She tells them that Willy has to work harder than ever since he is now paid on commission. Biff's comments on those 'ungrateful bastards' provokes this outburst from Linda:

> Are they any worse than his sons? When he brought them business, when he was young, they were glad to see him. But now, his old friends, the old buyers that loved him so and always found him some order to hand him a pinch—they're all dead, retired . . . and you tell me he has no character? The man who never worked a day but for your benefit? When does he get a medal for that? Is this his reward— to turn around at the age of sixty-three and find his sons, who he loved better than his life, one a philandering bum—. . . That's all you are, baby! (*To* BIFF) And you! What happened to the love you had for him? You were such pals! (p.45)

The sons now neglect him as much as the firm has done. Biff defends himself by saying that he knows Willy is a fake, but refuses to give any details. Linda then shocks them by saying that Willy is dying—that he has been trying to kill himself by crashing the car, as one witness in particular seemed to have observed: Linda comments:

> Well, it seems she was walking down the road and saw his car. She says that he wasn't driving fast at all, and that he didn't skid. She says he came to that little bridge, and then deliberately smashed into the railing, and it was only the shallowness of the water that saved him. (p.47)

Biff wants to dismiss this, but then Linda tells them that she has found a rubber pipe near the gas pipe in the cellar. Willy has placed it there to commit suicide by gassing himself. She has not told Willy that she knows, and appeals to Biff to help Willy: only he can do it. He promises to do so:

> LINDA: It sounds so old-fashioned and silly, but I tell you he put his whole life into you and you've turned your backs on him . . . Biff, I swear to God! Biff, his life is in your hands! . . .

BIFF: All right, pal, all right. It's settled now, I've been remiss. I know that, Mom. But I'll stay, and I swear to you, I'll apply myself. (*Kneeling in front of her, in a fever of self-reproach.*) It's just—you see, Mom, I don't fit in business. Not that I won't try. I'll try, and I'll make good. (p.47)

Biff then becomes angry with Happy for telling him that he will never make it in business as he once 'whistled in a elevator' when he worked before: an example of Biff's lack of self-discipline. This becomes important since Willy overhears this and also Biff's statement that the Loman family belong in the country, in the West where they can enjoy the open air. Willy, in turn, is angered. He asserts on his entry that he is not 'crazy' and that no one laughs at him—he is a 'Big shot'.

In an attempt to calm Willy, and change the subject, Happy tells him that Biff is due to see Bill Oliver to try to get a job, selling sporting goods. Willy immediately becomes interested, assuming that Biff already has the post. This provokes Biff's anger once more; the possibility of another argument occurs again. Happy intervenes once more, and suggests that the two brothers set up their own sporting business, with various teams used to advertise the goods. Willy is ecstatic over this idea. The subject now returns to the forthcoming interview with Oliver, with Willy giving advice; he tells Biff how much money to ask for, what to wear, how to project his personality. Willy resents Linda's interruptions and tells her so but this causes another argument as Biff tells Willy to stop 'yelling' at her. Willy leaves, hopeful for Biff. Linda asks Biff to try to be kind. Happy and Biff discuss the situation; Biff is determined to get the job with Oliver.

Willy and Linda are seen in the bedroom; Willy is confident that Biff will get the job; Biff assures Willy that everything will be all right. Willy goes to sleep dreaming about the past:

Like a young god. Hercules—something like that. And the sun, the sun all around him. Remember how he waved to me? Right up from the field, with the representatives of three colleges standing by? And the buyers I brought, and the cheers when he came out—Loman, Loman, Loman! God almighty, he'll be great yet. A star like that, magnificent, can never really fade away! (p.54)

This is one of the high points in Willy's belief in Biff's abilities; he compares his son to Hercules, in Greek legend the son of a god, and noted for his great strength.

Act two

This act opens at breakfast on the morning of Biff's interview. Willy is late for work but pleased that his sons have got away early and pleased also that Biff appeared eager. Willy once more seems keen on the idea of setting up a place in the country. Linda reminds him of their financial difficulties: the insurance premium is due, the car has had trouble, and the fridge is not paid for. They also have to repay the loan (mortgage) which has enabled them to purchase their house, in which they have lived for twenty-five years. They are 'behind' their repayments of the mortgage. Before Willy leaves, Linda tells him that the boys have arranged for the three of them to have a meal at Frank's Chop House. Willy departs on a note of optimism; while Linda is also convinced that 'It's changing, Willy, I can feel it changing!' (p.58).

Biff telephones to his mother; she tells him that the rubber tubing has gone, assuming that it is Willy himself who has removed it, but Biff informs her that he took it. Biff has not yet seen Oliver. Linda asks him to be kind to Willy, to act almost as he used to as a boy:

> Be loving to him. Because he's only a little boat looking for a harbour . . . Oh, that's wonderful, Biff, you'll save his life. Thanks, darling. Just put your arms around him when he comes into the restaurant. Give him a smile. (p.59)

The scene changes to Howard Wagner's office; he has a tape recorder and insists on playing back a recording of his daughter's voice to Willy. It is Howard's latest toy, costing only a hundred and fifty dollars, and Willy cannot resist saying that he will buy one, although the audience knows very well that he can't afford it.

Willy tells him the true purpose of his visit: he says that he doesn't want to travel any more, and would prefer to have a job in the town as had been mentioned by Wagner the previous Christmas. Wagner refuses, as they have no room. Willy asks for sixty-five dollars a week as a wage: he is tired and needs a job without travel. Wagner insists that there is still no room for him, and Willy comes down to fifty dollars a week. Willy then launches into a story of his ambitions to go to Alaska, how he first became a salesman, how he knew a very popular salesman who died a real death of a salesman by being liked by hundreds of people. Willy regrets that the old comradeship is missing: when he died, hundreds of salesmen and buyers were at his funeral:

> Things were said on a lotta trains for months after that . . . In those days there was personality in it, Howard. There was respect, and comradeship, and gratitude in it. Today, it's all cut and dried, and there's no chance for bringing friendship to bear—or personality. You see what I mean? They don't know me any more. (p.63-4)

He comes down to asking for forty dollars a week, and again Wagner refuses. Willy becomes agitated and reminds him of all the service he has put into the firm. After this, Wagner tells Willy that he no longer wishes Willy to represent the firm. He advises Willy to rest and return when he feels 'better'. Willy says that he needs the money, and Wagner suggests that he approaches his sons, but Willy is reluctant. Willy is left stunned and Wagner exits.

Ben now appears: again there is a scene from the past as re-enacted in Willy's mind. Ben has just finished a deal in Alaska, and he needs a man there to 'look after' things. Willy puts Ben's proposal to Linda, who is frightened by it and by Ben, and says that she thinks Willy has enough for her here and now. She reminds Willy that old Wagner (father of the Wagner who has just left the stage) has offered Willy some kind of partnership in the firm if he keeps up with the job; Willy agrees with this but Ben remains doubtful, as they have no material goods to prove their success. He tells Ben of the successful salesman, and of his popularity. Happy and Biff enter; Biff is ready for a football game, and Willy expresses his pride at his achievement:

> Without a penny to his name, three great Universities are begging for him, and from there the sky's the limit, because it's not what you do, Ben. It's who you know and the smile on your face! It's contacts, Ben, contacts! The whole wealth of Alaska passes over the lunch table at the Commodore Hotel, and that's the wonder, the wonder of this country, that a man can end with diamonds here on the basis of being liked! (*He turns to* BIFF.) And that's why when you get on that field today it's important. Because thousands of people will be rooting for you and loving you. (p.67–8)

It is necessary for Biff to succeed at the game to make people 'love' him. Ben leaves, reminding Willy that riches are on the doorstep.

Bernard enters, and Happy and he argue as to which of them shall carry Biff's helmet. Willy tells Biff how important the game is, as it is the Championship match. Charley enters and pretends not to know what is happening, to annoy Willy; he succeeds.

The scene moves back to the present (p.71). Bernard is now a young man, and a lawyer; he is going to Washington and has stopped to see Charley. He is also a sportsman and at the moment playing tennis. He is married and has settled, unlike Biff. Willy is surprised to see him and especially surprised to see the tennis rackets.

WILLY: (*small and alone*): What—what's the secret?
BERNARD: What secret?
WILLY: How—how did you? Why didn't he ever catch on?
BERNARD: I wouldn't know that, Willy.
WILLY: (*confidentially, desperately*): You were his friend, his boy-hood friend. There's something I don't understand about it. His life ended after that Ebbets Field game. From the age of seventeen nothing good ever happened to him. (p.72)

Bernard asks if Willy tried to persuade Biff to resit his failed math exam, and Willy insists that he did. He cannot understand why he refused. Bernard confirms that Biff had talked of retaking the exam but after a trip to Boston to see Willy his attitude changed. Bernard suspects that something happened to Biff in Boston and asks Willy. Charley enters and Bernard leaves for the train. Charley tells Willy that Bernard is to argue a case in the Supreme Court. Willy asks Charley for a loan of a hundred and ten dollars, after which Charley offers him a job for fifty dollars a week. Willy refuses this, claiming that he already has a job: his pride will not allow him to accept this from Charley now. Charley suspects that he is being insulted, but calmly accepts his position. Willy breaks down and reveals that he has just lost his job, but still refuses to accept Charley's offer. Charley is angered by this, but still agrees to lend him the money, pointing out to Willy that he is jealous of him. It occurs to Willy that he would be worth more dead than alive:

> Funny, y'know? After all the highways, and the trains and the appointments, and the years, you end up worth more dead than alive. (p.77)

The scene changes to the restaurant. Happy is making arrangements for the evening's dinner, and is then attracted by a girl who enters; he talks to her and engages her interest by giving her some champagne, which he pretends to sell for a living. Biff enters and is introduced to the girl, a Miss Forsyth. Happy continues with the chat and tells her that Biff is a professional football player. Happy makes a date with the girl and asks her to bring a friend. When she leaves, Biff proceeds with the serious conversation. He has been to Oliver's office, where he was kept waiting, and this has made him realise the truth about himself:

> Well, I waited six hours for him, see? All day. Kept sending my name in. Even tried to date his secretary so she'd get me to him, but no soap . . . Finally, about five o'clock he comes out . . . He walked away. I saw him for one minute. I got so mad I could've torn the wall down: How the hell did I ever get the idea I was a salesman there? I even believed myself that I'd been a salesman for him! And then he gave me one look and—I realized what a ridiculous lie my whole life has been. We've been talking in a dream for fifteen years. I was a shipping clerk . . . the next thing I know I'm in his office—panelled walls, everything. I can't explain it. I—Hap, I took his fountain pen. (p.82)

He realises that his life cannot be that of a salesman, and anyway he never was one before: he has been living in a dream, like the rest of the Lomans. He is determined to tell Willy what has happened, but Happy tries to persuade him not to do so, and to tell him a different story. This story is to be that Oliver has invited him to lunch the next day, and after that Biff can report that he is thinking it over. The subject can then be dropped. Willy enters the restaurant, and asks Biff how things went. Biff tries to explain the situation, beginning with the fact that he was once a shipping clerk and not really a salesman:

> 'I don't know who said it first, but I was never a salesman for Bill Oliver . . . Let's hold on to the facts, tonight, Pop. We're not going to get anywhere bullin' around. I was a shipping clerk'. (p.84)

Willy becomes angry at this and then reveals that he has been fired. Biff then begins the pretence that in fact he did see Oliver; Willy assumes that Oliver gave Biff a warm welcome. He won't allow Biff to finish his story, adding his own pieces, almost forcing Biff to lie:

> WILLY: Well, what happened? It's great news, Biff. Did he take you into his office or'd you talk in the waiting-room?
> BIFF: Well, he came in, see, and—
> WILLY: (*with a big smile*): What'd he say? Betcha he threw his arms around you.
> BIFF: Well, he kinda—
> WILLY: He's a fine man. (*To* HAPPY): Very hard man to see, y'know.
> HAPPY: (*agreeing*) Oh, I know.
> WILLY: (*To* BIFF): Is that where you had the drinks?
> BIFF: Yeah, he gave me a couple of—no, no!
> HAPPY: (*cutting in*): He told him my Florida idea.
> WILLY: Don't interrupt. (*To* BIFF): How'd he react the Florida idea?
> BIFF: Dad, will you give me a minute to explain? (p.85)

Biff finally has to say to Willy that he is not letting him tell Willy what he wants to. Willy becomes annoyed asking Biff if he insulted Oliver.

Young Bernard now enters, although this is in Willy's imagination. The action now is between Willy, his sons and Bernard. Willy converses with all three of them, although Biff and Happy know nothing of Bernard's 'presence'. For example, the obsession Willy has with the failed math exam arises, but Biff cannot understand what he is talking about:

> YOUNG BERNARD: (*frantically*): Mrs Loman, Mrs Loman!
> HAPPY: Tell him what happened!
> BIFF: (*To* HAPPY): Shut up and leave me alone!
> WILLY: No, no! You had to go and flunk math!
> BIFF: What math? What are you talking about?
> YOUNG BERNARD: Mrs Loman, Mrs Loman!
> WILLY: (*wildly*): Math, math, math!
> BIFF: Take it easy, Pop! (p.85–6)

Biff is determined to tell Willy the truth of the matter, that he waited for six hours without seeing Oliver. While he is attempting this, Bernard reveals that Biff has in fact failed his math exam, and that he has gone to Boston. The truth about Biff, and the stolen fountain pen, gradually penetrates to Willy and he becomes incoherent. In desperation, Biff says that he is due to see Oliver tomorrow; the incident with the pen can be explained away, according to Willy, but Biff remembers that he once stole some balls when he worked for Oliver before and he does not want to return. Willy becomes so angry that he strikes him, after Biff has revealed that he has no appointment in fact. This last incident is accompanied by the laughter of the Woman, a voice of conscience from Willy's past. (Compare the incident on page 30 with this.) The laughter is paralleled by the entry of the two girls. The Woman's voice is heard asking Willy to open the door, and Willy is about to obey the instruction but remembers where he is:

THE WOMAN: Willy, are you going to wake up?

BIFF: (*ignoring* WILLY): How're ya, miss, sit down. What do you drink?

MISS FORSYTHE: Letta might not be able to stay long.

LETTA: I gotta get up very early tomorrow. I got jury duty. I'm so excited! Were you fellows ever on a jury?

BIFF: No, but I been in front of them! (*The girls laugh*) This is my father.

LETTA: Isn't he cute? Sit down with us, Pop.

HAPPY: Sit him down, Biff!

BIFF: (*going to him*): Come on, slugger, drink us under the table. To hell with it! Come on, sit down, pal.

(*On* BIFF'S *last insistence,* WILLY *is about to sit.*)

THE WOMAN: (*Now urgently*): Willy, are you going to answer the door!

(THE WOMAN'S *call pulls* WILLY *back. He starts right, befuddled:*)

BIFF: Hey, where are you going?

WILLY: Open the door.

BIFF: The door?

WILLY: The washroom . . . the door . . . where's the door? (p.89–90)

Willy leaves for the washroom. Happy and Biff argue, each accusing the other of not caring about Willy. They are aware that Willy is a potential suicide case.

As they leave, the scene changes so that we learn about the significance of the Woman. She is a figure from Willy's past, and the scene is set in the past. They are sharing a hotel room, during Willy's travels in Boston. Young Biff finds him: he has come to tell Willy that he has failed his math exam. At this point, Biff does not know about the

existence of the Woman, they do not seem to take the failure very
seriously and joke about the teacher concerned:

> BIFF: See, the reason he hates me, Pop—one day he was late for
> class so I got up at the blackboard and imitated him. I
> crossed my eyes and talked with a lithp.
>
> WILLY: (*laughing*): You did? The kids like it?
>
> BIFF: They nearly died laughing!
>
> WILLY: Yeah? What'd you do?
>
> BIFF: The thquare root of thixthy twee is . . . (p.93)

They both laugh at this. The Woman, offstage, joins in the laughter.
Willy tries to conceal the fact that she is there. She enters, joking; Willy
tries to get rid of her, but she is persistent, and it becomes obvious that
Willy is staying with her:

> WILLY: Ah—you better go back to your room. They must be
> finished painting by now. They're painting her room so
> I let her take a shower in here. Go back, go back . . . (*He
> pushes her*)
>
> THE WOMAN: (*resisting*): But I've got to get dressed, Willy, I can't—
>
> WILLY: Get out of here! Go back, go back . . . (*suddenly striving
> for the ordinary*). This is Miss Francis, Biff, she's a
> buyer. They're painting her room . . . (p.94)

Biff is upset and cries; Willy tries to explain away the situation by saying
that she is just a 'buyer', and that anyway he gets very lonely. Biff has
no sympathy and accuses Willy of being a 'fake':

> WILLY: She's nothing to me, Biff. I was lonely, I was terribly lonely.
>
> BIFF: You—you gave her Mama's stockings! (*His tears break
> through and he rises to go.*)
>
> WILLY: (*grabbing for* BIFF): I gave you an order!
>
> BIFF: Don't touch me you—liar!
>
> WILLY: Apologize for that!
>
> BIFF: You fake! You phony little fake! You fake! (p.94-5)

Overcome, he leaves, with Willy calling after him. The scene now moves
back to the present, in the restaurant. Willy is still confused, and leaves,
talking about having to buy 'seeds'.

There is another change of scene, this time to the house. Linda is
annoyed at Happy and Biff, who seem to have a flippant attitude towards Willy, little caring whether he lives or dies; she accuses them of
'deserting' Willy in the restaurant for a couple of 'whores'. While Happy
leaves, Biff stays to collect the flowers that Happy has dropped and he
refuses to take Linda's advice; he says the time for an 'abrupt conversation' (p.95) has arrived. But Willy is planting the garden; he is appar-

ently deranged, but he is talking to Ben about the insurance policies and his premium. He has a policy which matures on his death for twenty thousand dollars. He speaks of a grand funeral, just like the other salesman had:

> WILLY: . . . Because he thinks I'm nothing, see, and so he spites me. But the funeral—(*Straightening up*) Ben, the funeral will be massive! They'll come from Maine, Massachusetts, Vermont, New Hampshire! All the old-timers with the strange licence plates—the boy will be thunderstruck, Ben, because he never realised—I am known! . . . and he'll see it with his eyes once and for all. (p.100)

This is the only thing that Willy has left to give Biff. Biff enters and tells Willy that he is leaving, that he has no appointment with Oliver. He asks him to come with him to tell Linda that he is leaving, but Willy is reluctant. Biff tries to shake hands, to say goodbye in a friendly manner, but Willy accuses him of spite. Willy cannot be placated, using such terms as 'May you rot in hell if you leave this house' (p.103). He tells Biff not to blame him when things go wrong; Biff now loses his temper, calls Willy a phony, brings the rubber tube from his pocket, but Willy denies all knowledge of it:

> BIFF: All right, phony! Then let's lay it on the line. (*He whips the rubber tube out of his pocket and puts it on the table.*)
> HAPPY: You crazy—
> LINDA: Biff! . . .
> BIFF: Leave it there! Don't move it!
> WILLY: (*not looking at it*): What is that?
> BIFF: You know goddam well what it is.
> WILLY: (*caged, wanting to escape*): I never saw that!
> BIFF: You saw it. The mice didn't bring it into the cellar! What is this supposed to do, make a hero out of you? This supposed to make me sorry for you? (p.103)

Biff has decided that it is time the truth was told in the Loman house for once. He says that all of them are pretending to be something they're not; Willy has filled him with 'hot air'; he must realise that Biff is a low character, that he has stolen and that he has been in jail. He, like Willy, is a 'dime a dozen' (p.105), and both must realise it. He finally breaks down in tears, and leaves to go to bed. Willy's interpretation of this is that 'he likes me' (p.106), because he has cried in his presence. Willy confirms, through the supposed presence of Ben, that Biff deserves the insurance money, and he is determined to give it to him. Linda is worried and calls for Willy to come to bed, but he remains 'discussing' the matter with Ben; he is happy that Biff likes him. He goes to the car, drives off and crashes, killing himself. The act ends with the funeral procession.

Requiem

The funeral rites. Linda cannot understand 'why' it had to happen, since they were becoming financially sound. Biff is uncompromising, saying that Willy had all the wrong dreams and that he never knew himself. Happy has the idea of the 'Loman brothers' still, but Biff knows that it is not possible.

Linda is left alone, talking over Willy's grave, and on the words 'we're free' the play ends.

Part 3

Commentary

MILLER SAW the play as 'setting forth what happens when a man does not have a proper grip on the forces of life'. He also regarded the play as a modern tragedy—a play which shows that, despite the apparent ordinariness of everyday life, one man can still attain heroic proportions. The question arises as to whether Willy ever does become heroic, and whether the play ever reaches the tragic heights that Miller hoped it would. Miller, in an essay entitled *Tragedy and the Common Man**, wrote that 'tragic feeling is evoked in us when we are in the presence of a character who is ready to lay down his life, if need be, to secure one thing—his sense of personal dignity'. Now, this differs from the traditional view of tragedy and the feelings evoked in the audience by a tragic hero in that, formerly, the tragic hero was a man above other men, one who rose above the ordinary, and one who was struggling against a seemingly invincible fate; the character also had one major failing—his 'tragic flaw'—that brought about his downfall. One of the problems with *Death of a Salesman* is, then, how successful Miller has been in transforming Willy, the ordinary man, into a modern hero, one who acquires dignity, and one who, we feel, rises above the challenges of society while at the same time facing and responding to them. Does Willy deserve our sympathy? Is Miller's definition a satisfactory one and how far is it a definition contrived to fit the play, rather than a broad definition applicable to more than one play?

Another aspect of the play is the view that Willy has of the United States; he sees it as a land of opportunity in which ambitious young people like Biff can accomplish great things. Yet, in reality, America does not seem to conform to this view; America, although it may be still a land of opportunity, seems to have acquired a new set of values. Just what these values are, and how Willy sets about dealing with them, represent a comment on the society. The most significant of all the relationships between the characters in the play is the one between Willy and Biff. Biff is undoubtedly the favourite, and yet he cannot live up to what Willy wants for him, nor can he really share Willy's ambitions for the future. Willy is unable to convince him, and Biff is unable to respond. They seem unable to communicate. It is a gap of the generations between father and son, a gap of ideals and one which Willy

*Included in *American Playwrights on Drama*, ed. Frenz Horst, Hill and Wang, New York, 1965, pp.79–83.

comes to see as the play progresses. Connected with this gap is the acquisition of self-knowledge by both Willy and Biff. They both have to come to terms with themselves, the one with the fact that his son is not ambitious, the other with facing up to the 'fake' existence that he insists the Lomans lead, and with attempting to make the rest of the family see it also. 'Ambitions' and 'reality' are perhaps the two key words here.

Society

The play is set in twentieth-century industrial society, complete with apartment blocks, financial difficulties and pressures to succeed. Money defines success: people are judged by the amount they acquire, and the amount of success is linked with the amount of money they have. Since the play is about city life there are frequent references to money and the worries which it brings:

LINDA: Did you sell anything?

WILLY: I did five hundred gross in Providence and seven hundred gross in Boston.

LINDA: No!... That makes your commission ... Two hundred—my God! Two hundred and twelve dollars!

WILLY: Well, I didn't figure it out yet, but ...

LINDA: How much did you do?

WILLY: ... roughly two hundred on the whole trip ... What do we owe?

LINDA: Well, on the first there's sixteen dollars on the refrigerator—

WILLY: Why sixteen?

LINDA: Well, the fan belt broke, so it was a dollar eighty ... there's nine sixty for the washing machine. And for the vacuum cleaner there's three and a half due on the fifteenth. Then the roof, you got twenty-one dollars remaining ... odds and ends, comes to around a hundred and twenty dollars by the fifteenth. (p.27-8)

There is nothing trivial about this: Willy feels he has to succeed, and the only way to show his success is to acquire money and material goods. He does not want to face the fact that he is not earning enough. The scene quoted above can be paralleled by the following quotation in Act Two, which shows the pressures of what is sometimes called the consumer society, where pressures of advertising persuade people to acquire goods, and to do so by paying for them by instalments:

WILLY: I told you we should've bought a well-advertised machine. Charley bought a General Electric and its twenty years old and it's still good, that son-of-a-bitch.

LINDA: But, Willy—

WILLY: Whoever heard of a Hastings refrigerator? Once in my life I would like to own something outright before it's broken! I'm always in a race with the junkyard! I just finished paying for the car and it's on its last legs. The refrigerator consumes belts like a goddam maniac. They time those things. They time those things. They time them so when you finally paid for them, they're used up. (p.56-7)

Willy is disturbed by the element of rapid obsolescence which is a highly oppressive aspect of life. There are however two types of society represented in the play. The modern consumer society described in the quotation above is contrasted with the countryside; the structure of the society there is much simpler and different, the image of an older America. Biff needs to escape to it, to enjoy the pleasures of nature without modern pressure. But this is only a dream, and the realities of modern life dominate:

WILLY: The street is lined with cars. There's not a breath of fresh air in the neighbourhood. The grass don't grow any more, you can't raise a carrot in the backyard. They should've had a law against apartment houses. Remember those two beautiful elm trees out there? When Biff and I hung the swing between them? . . . they should've arrested the builder for cutting those down. They massacred the neighbourhood. (*Lost*) More and more I think of those days, Linda. This time of year it was lilac and wistaria. (p.12)

Willy is not typical of society—he feels he has to be within it, yet looks back to a golden age when life was simpler. The society in which the Lomans live is governed by people like Ben—ruthless managers who care little for the opinions of others, and in such a society the Lomans, although they only occasionally realise it, are out of place.

Character analysis

Willy

Willy Loman is introduced immediately to the reader as someone who is 'exhausted'. As he enters the house at the begining of the play, Miller makes it clear that he should be seen as a man whose 'exhaustion is apparent' (p.8). Yet we are also told that he is a man of dreams, 'massive dreams', and someone who finds hope for the future in those dreams. Part of his dream is one of the beauty of nature, in complete contrast to the realities of his mundane existence: he says that he has forgotten about the road and driving and has observed the scenery:

> it's so beautiful up there, Linda, the trees are so thick, and the sun is warm. I opened the windshield and just let the warm air bathe over me . . . (p.9)

But he also sees himself as vital to the trade of New England, which is his territory for selling; any move or demotion would be an affront to his pride. Part of his pride is the pride of being a Loman, a pride that he hopes all of the family will share. Any Loman who does not share his dreams and ambitions has let him down. Biff has always been his favourite, but Willy finds something lacking in him:

> WILLY: How can he find himself on a farm? Is that a life? A farm-hand? In the beginning, when he was young, I thought, well, a young man, it's good for him to tramp round, take a lot of different jobs, but it's more than ten years now and he has yet to make thirty-five dollars a week!
>
> LINDA: He's finding himself, Willy.
>
> WILLY: Not finding yourself at the age of thirty-four is a disgrace!
>
> LINDA: Shh!
>
> WILLY: The trouble is, he's lazy, goddamit! . . . Biff is a lazy bum!

This attitude does not last long, however, for Willy believes in Biff and believes he is a man of quality:

> WILLY: Biff Loman is lost. In the greatest country in the world a young man with such—personal attractiveness gets lost. And such a hard worker. There's one thing about Biff—he's not lazy . . . I'll see him in the morning; I'll have a nice talk with him. I'll get him a job selling. He could be big in no time. My God! Remember how they used to follow him around in high school? When he smiled at one of them their faces lit up.
>
> (p.11)

Willy bases this opinion on his past knowledge of Biff, from Biff's school-days. But Biff is now thirty-four, and without regular work. Willy seems unable to face the fact that Biff will never become a great man.

Everything that brings joy to Willy is associated with the past; he complains (p.12) that they are 'boxed in' and that there is no longer any room for them. Connected with the past are memories of Biff. He remembers 'how Biff used to simonize [a proprietary brand of car polish] the car. The dealer refused to believe there was eighty thousand miles on it' (p.13). Biff and Happy have given him pleasure; the simpler life associated to some extent with nature has given him that also.

Willy's hopes are so closely associated with Biff that he seems unable to remember for long that Biff is a mature man, supposedly capable of making his own decisions. He has the same attitude towards Biff in the present as he used to have in the past, when he could play the role of the father-figure successfully. What he says about finding Biff a job is very like a man talking about his young son; he advised Biff in the past just as he tries to advise him in the present:

> WILLY: I been wondering why you polish the car so careful. Ha! don't leave the hubcaps, boys. Get the chamois to the hubcaps. Happy, use newspapers on the windows, it's the easiest thing, show him how to do it, Biff! You see, Happy? Pad it up, use it like a pad, that's it, that's it, good work. You're doin' all right, Hap . . . Biff, first thing we gotta do when we find time is clip that big branch over the house . . . (p.21)

This return to the past in Willy's mind occurs because the family is all-important to him and partly because he is becoming deranged: as the play progresses we see him come to the conclusion that life is not worth living, that he and the family would be better if he were dead. The past can never be reclaimed. In the past, Willy has been able to impress his sons, to convince them—and himself—of the great worth of selling and of his own personal esteem:

> BIFF: Where'd you go this time Dad? Gee, we were lonesome for you.
> WILLY: (*pleased, puts an arm around each boy and they come down to the apron*): Lonesome, heh?
> BIFF: Missed you every minute.
> WILLY: Don't say? Tell you a secret, boys. Don't breathe it to a soul. Someday I'll have my own business, and I'll never have to leave home any more.
> HAPPY: Like Uncle Charley, heh?
> WILLY: Bigger than Uncle Charley! Because Charley is not—liked. He's liked, but not—well liked.
> BIFF: Where'd you go this time, Dad?
> WILLY: Well, I got on the road, and I went north to Providence. Met the Mayor.
> BIFF: The Mayor of Providence!
> WILLY: He was sitting in the hotel lobby.
> BIFF: What'd he say?
> WILLY: He said 'Morning!' And I said, 'You got a fine city here, Mayor.' And then he had coffee with me . . . (p.23)

Here Willy expresses one of his basic beliefs that it is necessary to be liked. Willy says that to succeed in business is a matter of personality; the gift is to be able to convince customers of one's own worth. This is an idea reiterated several times in the play (see, for example, p.51), and one which is dear to Willy. It is also one which is shown to be false. He assumes Biff has the same personal charm and appeal that he supposes he has himself, which will ensure success in later life:

> WILLY: Bernard can get the best marks in school, y'understand, but when he gets out in the business world, y'understand, you are going to be five times ahead of him. That's why I thank God Almighty you're both built like Adonises. Because the man who makes an appearance in the business world, the man who creates personal interest, is the man who gets ahead. Be liked and you will never want. (p.25-6)

Willy again misjudges the situation.

Earlier, the gradual decline in the state of Willy's mind was mentioned. We are prepared for this, not only by the flashbacks, but also by the little inconsistencies which he displays. For example, Willy says of his car that it is 'the greatest car ever built' (p.26), while a few moments later he changes to 'that goddam Chevrole, they ought to prohibit the manufacture of that car' (p.28). These scenes take place in the past, showing that Willy has always been a figure of several faces, in all of which he believes: to the boys, he must be the successful father, to Linda the provider, and to himself the great salesman. He realises, though, that he is not the great salesman that he pretends to be:

> WILLY: I gotta be at it ten, twelve hours a day. Other men—I don't know—they do it easier. I don't know why—I can't stop myself? I talk too much. A man oughta come in with a few words. One thing about Charley. He's man of few words, and they respect him. (p.28)

He cannot understand Charley's success. His own formula seems to have broken down under comparison, and yet he can never admit this. He needs to believe in himself in order to survive. His values are the values of old; he dreams of the paradise open to a great salesman:

> WILLY: . . . I met a salesman in the Parker House. His name was Dave Singleman. And he was eighty-four years old, and he'd drummed merchandise in thirty-one states. And old Dave, he'd go to his room, y'understand, put on his green velvet slippers—I'll never forget—and pick up his phone and call the buyers, and without leaving his room, at the age of eighty-four, he made his living. And when I saw that, I realized that selling was the greatest career a man could want. (p.63)

Significantly, Willy remarks that this took place 'in those days', but they have now gone. Willy is a salesman who is attempting to use those values in a society in which, to be really successful, the advice of Ben is standard: 'never fight fair with a stranger, boy', he remarks to Biff (p.38), 'you'll never get out of the jungle that way'. The winner is the ruthless aggressor, which Willy is not capable of becoming.

On several occasions, Willy mentions that he is a lonely man. While he is on the road he says that he needs Linda (p.29) and this leads to the affair with the Woman. When Biff discovers the truth, Willy again says how 'lonely' he is; the Woman is simply for company, but this is not the whole truth. The Woman has made him feel wanted, has made him feel as though he were *the* salesman that he imagines himself as being:

THE WOMAN: . . . When'll you be back?
WILLY: Oh, two weeks about. Will you come up again?
THE WOMAN: Sure thing. You do make me laugh. It's good for me . . . And I think you're a wonderful man. (p.30)

WILLY: I'm so lonely.
THE WOMAN: You know you ruined me, Willy? From now on, when-ever you come to the office, I'll see that you go through to the buyers. No waiting at my desk any more, Willy. You ruined me.
WILLY: That's nice of you to say that. (p.92)

Willy's longing to be seen as a successful man and to be placed in a position where he can reach all the top buyers is obviously connected with the affair with the Woman, while it also reveals the superficiality of his family life: his concern for Linda and the boys is genuine, but his need for success overcomes his feelings of loyalty. He is also tied emotionally to Biff, Happy and Linda, but he is tied to his work emotionally also. When Howard Wagner explains to Willy that he cannot work on the floor and, finally, that he has lost his job, Willy becomes desperate:

WILLY: . . . There were promises made across this desk! You mustn't tell me you've got people to see—I put thirty-four years into this firm, Howard, and now I can't pay my insurance! You can't eat the orange and throw the peel away—a man is not a piece of fruit! (*After a pause*) Now pay attention. Your father—in 1928 I had a big year. I averaged a hundred and seventy dollars a week in com-missions.
HOWARD: (*impatiently*): Now, Willy, you never averaged . . . (p.64)

Money once more defines success; by losing his job, Willy has let every-one down, most of all himself. What Willy has to be is 'a man'. Home-building and providing for the family is part of a man's duty; without a job, Willy can do neither. His pride is hurt.

Pride is a strong element in Willy's character. The house he has been paying for over the past twenty-five years has been cared for by him and reconstructed by him; he is proud of his work:

LINDA: ... After this payment, Willy, the house belongs to us.

WILLY: It's twenty-five years!

LINDA: Biff was nine years old when we bought it.

WILLY: Well, that's a great thing. To weather a twenty-five-year mortgage is—

LINDA: It's an accomplishment.

WILLY: All the cement, the lumber, the reconstruction I put in this house! There ain't a crack to be found in it any more. (p.57)

The work remains incomplete, however, while Biff will not accept his responsibilities. Willy is proud of being a successful salesman, or, rather, of giving the appearance of being one. This is why he is insulted when Charley offers him a job (p.33), and why, after he has lost his job, he cannot work for Charley (p.76–7).

In the past, Charley has been seen as an example of a meek man, different from the Lomans, a man who will never be really truly successful, despite Willy's admission on p.28 (quoted above, p.31). Part of the contradictory nature of Willy is revealed by the acceptance of yet another loan from Charley: he can accept the 'charity' but cannot accept the supposed hurt to his pride that a job might inflict upon him. Charley's assertion that Willy has been 'jealous' of him all his life (p.77) is probably true, but Willy is only just becoming fully aware of it. By giving us occasional glimpses into the past, Miller reveals Willy's subconscious: Charley is right, Willy has been jealous, but frightened to admit it openly. Charley also helps to break down Willy's belief that to be well liked is the most important quality in a salesman:

CHARLEY: Willy, when're gonna realize that them things don't mean anything? You named him Howard, but you can't sell that. The only thing you got in this world is what you can sell. And the funny thing is that you're a salesman, and you don't know that.

WILLY: I've always tried to think otherwise, I guess. I always felt that if a man was impressive, and well liked, that nothing—

CHARLEY: Why must everybody like you? Who liked J.P. Morgan? Was he impressive? In a Turkish bath he'd look like a butcher. But with his pockets on he was well liked.
(p.76–7)

The scene closes with Willy's statement that Charley is the best friend he ever had. Certainly, Willy learns more about himself in this speech from Charley than from anyone else at this stage in the play.

The chief source of Willy's pride is Biff. In his school days, Biff was a successful sportsman. Willy lives for the day when he will have the world at his feet; winning a football game isn't an isolated incident:

> WILLY: . . . that's the wonder, the wonder of this country when a man can end with diamonds here on the basis of being liked! (*He turns to* BIFF.) And that's why when you get out on that field today it's important. Because thousands of people will be rooting for you and loving you. . . . And Ben! when he walks into a business office his name will sound out like a bell and all the doors will open to him: I've seen it, Ben, I've seen it a thousand times! You can't feel it in your hand like timber, but it's there! (p.68)

This speech is significant for it reveals several facets of Willy's character. The universities, he says earlier, are 'begging' for Biff; 'contacts' are the clue to success, and America is once again seen as 'wonderful'. Personality means not just support from the crowd at a football game, but support in business circles in later life. To Willy the game becomes a symbol for success in the future. Even after Willy has lost his job, he still takes consolation in the possibility of Biff regaining a lucrative position with Bill Oliver. Willy has forgotten that Biff never did have such a position—he was merely a shipping clerk. Willy does not listen to Biff: he is not interested in the truth, merely in confirming what he suspects and hopes Biff to be: he asks and expects to be told that Oliver gave him a warm welcome, that he gave him drinks, that he accepted the ideas which Biff had. As Biff says (p.86), 'Dad, you're not letting me tell you what I want to tell you'. Biff is trying to impress reality upon Willy, but Willy is simply interested in the dream.

After Willy learns the truth, his life becomes meaningless. Although he still feels that he has to provide for his family, he can no longer do so from his work, so the idea of suicide occurs to him, because if he dies the money from his insurance policy will provide financial support for his family. Even at this stage, Biff is at the centre of his thoughts: he will be able to use the money to secure a good future for himself:

> WILLY: You gotta consider, now. Don't answer so quick. Remember, it's a guaranteed twenty-thousand dollar proposition. Now look, Ben, I want you to go through the inside and outs of this thing with me. I've got nobody to talk to, Ben, and the woman has suffered, you hear me? (p.99–100)

This occurs in the play before the confrontation with Biff, in which Willy interprets Biff's anger and his crying as a sign of affection; 'Isn't that remarkable? Biff—he likes me!' he says in response. This speech leaves no doubts in his mind: his gesture will be final, but it will be the one that will make Biff magnificent. True, Willy is deranged at this point, but his action is not a single moment of madness. It is the culmination of all that has happened during the play—and, remember, the action goes back several years. The exhausted, idealistic man who had visions of a great future for his sons does not in the end come to terms with reality, but retains his hopes. To Willy, death is the only answer.

Finally, some mention needs to be made of Willy's self-deception. Throughout the play he is a man who is portrayed as someone who cannot face up to reality. Even when he is presented with it, as in the case of the final confrontation with Biff, he reinterprets it to make it conform to his own needs. When faced with the fact that he is no longer useful as a salesman, he avoids considering the reasons for his failure, insisting instead that he used to be the best; the speech already quoted on page 64 reveals this. And when he says to Bernard (p.72) that Oliver is interested in Biff for a big financial deal, we see again this need to keep up a facade. Willy is self-deceived since he refuses to face up to the truth about himself and about his family. Despite this, Willy is liked by the characters in the play. Charley, although laughed at by Willy earlier, frequently lends him money; Bernard tries to talk to him. Moreover, his sons still show some affection for him, and Linda admires him. He never attains the heights to which he aspires, but, despite his weaknesses, his friends and family attempt to understand and help him. Biff's comment that 'he never really knew who he was' (p.111) is apt, but as Charley adds 'Nobody dast blame this man'.

Biff

Biff, in Linda's words, has not found himself, despite his mature years. He has a 'worn air' and is less self-assured than his brother Happy. His lack of self-assurance stems from two things, we are told: the uncertainty about his father's attitude towards him, and his doubts about his own life and future:

> HAPPY: . . . what happened, Biff? Where's the old humour, the old confidence? (*He shakes* BIFF'S *knee.* BIFF *gets up and moves restlessly about the room.*) What's the matter?
> BIFF: Why does dad mock me all the time?
> HAPPY: He's not mocking you, he—
> BIFF: Everything I say there's a twist of mockery on his face. I can't get near him.
> HAPPY: He just wants you to make good, that's all. (p.15)

Happy cannot understand the change in Biff, while Biff cannot make sense of their father. The two are connected, as will be seen later.

Biff has spent most of his time drifting from job to job. He is satisfied neither with life in the city, nor with life in the country:

> BIFF: . . . it's a measly manner of existence. To get on that subway on the hot mornings in the summer. To devote your whole life to keeping stock, or making phone calls, or selling or buying. To suffer fifty weeks of the year for the sake of a two-week vacation, when all you really desire is to be outdoors, with your shirt off. And always to have to be ahead of the next fella . . . Texas is cool now and it's spring. And whenever spring comes to where I am, I suddenly get the feeling, my God, I'm not getting anywhere. What the hell am I doing, playing around with horses, twenty-eight dollars a week! I'm thirty-four years old, I ought to be making my future. (p.16–17)

Biff is a man who has not found his place in society, but he also realises that he does not fit into any of the openings that society has made. Now, this represents a great change in Biff. Formerly, he knew his position. Encouraged by his father, Biff was a good sportsman at school, popular, and the star of the side: the 'flashback' scenes present Biff as the local football hero, admired by his brother and his friends. He is also seen as genuinely admiring Willy: he asserts that he misses him when he goes on his business trips, and believes in Willy's dream. At this stage in his life, Biff conformed to Willy's idea of what he should be; he was liked, good at 'manly' things like football, and hopeful for the future. He is contrasted with Bernard in some of these points; Willy describes Bernard as an 'anaemic'. Biff will succeed because of prowess; Bernard's success in the academic world of school will mean nothing in the future:

> WILLY: Don't be a pest, Bernard! (*To his boys*) What an anaemic!
> BERNARD: Okay, I'm waiting for you in my house, Biff . . .
> WILLY: Bernard is not well liked, is he?
> BIFF: He's liked, but he's not well liked.
> HAPPY: That's right, Pop.
> WILLY: That's just what I mean, Bernard can get the best marks in school, y'understand, but when he gets out in the business world, y'understand, you are going to be five times ahead of him. That's why I thank Almighty God you're both built like Adonises. Because the man who makes an appearance in the business world, the man who creates a personal interest, is the man who gets ahead. (p.25)

Biff believes this and is determined to succeed in these terms. The close relationship between Biff and his father is a sign of the enthusiasm for life that Biff once had. His attitude goes through a dramatic change. When we see Biff in the present, we see a man unsure of himself, unsure of Willy and unsure of the relationship with him; it is an attitude that Linda cannot understand: she also tries to emphasise the gravity of Biff's own position:

LINDA: . . . Why are you so hateful to each other? Why is that?
BIFF: (*evasively*): I'm not hateful, Mom.
LINDA: But you no sooner come in the door than you're fighting!
BIFF: I don't know why, I mean to change. I'm tryin', Mom; you understand?
LINDA: Are you home to stay now?
BIFF: I don't know. I want to look around, see what's doin'.
LINDA: Biff, you can't look around all your life, can you?
BIFF: I just can't take hold, Mom. I can't take hold of some kind of life. (p.42)

He has not, of course, changed towards his mother: she remains the 'old pal' that she has always been. It is Linda who reveals to him that Willy has been trying to kill himself, and that only Biff can help. 'Biff, his life is in your hands!' she exclaims (p.47).

Biff, however, is never able to bring himself to pretend to be able to win in the business world. He is too undisciplined and he has been too disillusioned by Willy's past to want to have anything to do with it. He has come to realise that the Lomans simply 'don't belong' in the city, that their life should be lived outside the city, away from the rat-race:

BIFF: I don't care what they think! They've laughed at Dad for years, and you know why? Because we don't belong in this nuthouse of a city. We should be mixing cement on some open plain, or — or carpenters. A carpenter is allowed to whistle! (p.48)

Like Willy earlier, he sees the city as a concrete jungle; unlike Willy, he refuses to conform to the demands of the city.

His admiration for Willy does lead him into trying for the job with Bill Oliver, a job for which he has little enthusiasm, but one which he feels obliged to apply for on the basis of Willy's decline and his need for Biff's support. He has some initial enthusiasm, after Happy's suggestion that they could set up a sports centre, but this enthusiasm quickly wanes when he realises just what he is and what he is capable of. In fact, the interview he hopes for with Oliver never takes place. While waiting to see him he realises what his situation is—that he has been dreaming of success, but that the dream has no basis in reality:

HAPPY: Did you tell him my Florida idea?

BIFF: He walked away. I saw him for one minute. I got so mad I could've torn the walls down! How the hell did I ever get the idea that I was a salesman there? I even believed myself that I'd been a salesman for him! And then he gave me one look and—I realized what a ridiculous lie my whole life has been. We've been talking in dreams for fifteen years. I was a shipping clerk. (p.82)

He cannot keep up the pretence; and, just as several years ago he stole from Oliver, he does the same thing in the office by taking the fountain pen, an action which he cannot explain. Biff is forced to stall even longer before he tells Willy exactly how he feels, for Willy reveals that he has just lost his job; even when he does tell Willy about the pen, he finds himself incapable of telling him the complete truth. The only thing for him to do is to leave. He decides to go, hoping Willy will accept it quietly, or even forget him:

BIFF: . . . I'm going and I'm not writing any more . . . People ask me where I am and what I'm doing, you don't know, and you don't care. That way it'll be off your mind and you can start brightening up again. All right? That clears it doesn't it? (WILLY *is silent, and* BIFF *goes to him.*) You gonna wish me luck, scout? (*He extends his hand*) What do you say? (p.102)

Biff has obviously misjudged Willy's nature. Willy is so involved that he could never allow Biff to leave without some explanation. Biff is provoked and the truth erupts:

BIFF: No! Nobody's hanging himself, Willy! I ran down eleven flights with a pen in my hand today. And suddenly I stopped, you hear me? And in the middle of that office building, do you hear this? I stopped in the middle of that building and I saw— the sky. I saw the things that I love in this world. The work and the food and the time to sit and smoke. And I looked at the pen and said to myself, what the hell am I grabbing this for? Why am I trying to become what I don't want to be? What am I doing in an office, making a contemptuous, begging fool of myself, when all I want is out there, waiting for me the minute I say I know who I am! Why can't I say that, Willy? (p.105)

At this moment Biff sees himself as the exponent of 'truth'; for the first time, his pent-up emotions are released and he comes to terms with what he really wants. One of the things that has happened to Biff is that he has been confronted by life in the city; he has rejected it in favour of the simpler, although less lucrative life in the country. At the beginning

of the play he had remarked in a conversation with Happy that he didn't
know which path to choose; by this stage in the play's action he has
decided, rejecting the city life in favour of the country. He is full of
bitterness because he sees that he and the rest of the family have led a
false existence; the time has arrived to face up to reality.

It was mentioned earlier that Biff's attitude towards Willy changed
during the years from schooldays to the present. As a schoolboy, just
before he was due to enter university, he loved and admired Willy. The
discovery that Willy was having an affair with 'the Woman' brings
home the truth to Biff; his words are significant:

BIFF: I'm not going there.
WILLY: Heh? If I can't get him to change that mark you'll make it
         up in summer school. You've got all summer to—
BIFF: (*His weeping breaking from him*): Dad—. . .
WILLY: She's nothing to me, Biff. I was lonely, I was terribly lonely.
BIFF: You—you gave her Mama's stockings! (*His tears break
         through and he rises to go*)
WILLY: (*grabbing for* BIFF): I gave an order!
BIFF: Don't touch me, you—liar!
WILLY: Apologize for that!
BIFF: You fake! you phony little fake! you fake! (p.95)

Biff never recovers from this discovery of Willy's falsity: the emotional
support has been removed. Willy is fallible and Biff has been brought
shockingly into contact with this fact. The belief he now has that Willy
is a 'fake' stays with him and accounts for his decline, for his realisation
that city life as a whole can be a fake and involves deceit—as with the
pretence necessary in the attempted interview with Oliver. He never
reveals what he knows, but it produces a profound effect within him,
the result of which is, in Willy's terms, 'laziness', and a refusal to conform to a particular image. He could be blamed for allowing Willy to
die, but he refuses to live a lie; for him, the dream is dead and the reality
of everyday life must be faced.

Happy

Happy has very much more confidence than Biff. Like his brother he
is lost, but in a very different way, for he has never allowed himself
to turn his face toward defeat (p.11). He has tried to conform to the
demands of the city, and is a moderate success. He likes to think of
himself as more than he actually is, and it is not until Biff's outburst
(p.104) that his real position is revealed: he is 'one of the two assistants
to the assistant'. He perseveres with his job, hoping for promotion:
he is committed to conform, despite his loneliness within the system:

HAPPY: . . . All I can do now is wait for the merchandise manager to die. And suppose I get to be merchandise manager? He's a good friend of mine, and he just built a terrific estate on Long Island. And he lived there about two months and sold it, and now he's building another one. He can't enjoy it once it's finished. And I know that's just what I would do. I don't know what the hell I'm workin' for, sometimes I sit in my apartment—all alone. And I think of the rent I'm paying. And it's crazy. But then, it's what I always wanted. My own apartment, a car, and plenty of women. And still, goddammit, I'm lonely. (p.17)

Like Biff and Willy, he has not found himself, but he has the apparent compensation of material possessions.

He is enthusiastic about Biff's idea to 'make it out West', and by his own suggestion that 'the Loman brothers' can set up a business selling sporting goods. Now, these two ideas are not compatible: the former demands a life in the country while the latter demands a dedication to the sort of life he already leads, and which Willy already leads. The latter idea seems to take precedence with him, however, since what he needs is success, to be respected and to reach the top:

HAPPY: I gotta show some of those pompous self-important executives over there that Hap Loman can make the grade. I want to walk into the store the way he walks in. Then I'll go with you, Biff. We'll be together yet, I swear. (p.18)

In fact, Happy's need for power is given more forceful expression a few lines later:

HAPPY: . . . that girl I was with tonight is engaged to be married in five weeks . . . [to the president of the store]. I don't know what gets into me, maybe I just have an over-developed sense of competition or something, but I went and ruined her, and furthermore I can't get rid of her. And he's the third executive I've done that to. Isn't that a crummy characteristic? And to top it all, I go to their weddings! . . . Like I'm not supposed to take bribes. Manufacturers offer me a hundred-dollar bill now and then to throw an order their way. You know how honest I am, but it's like this girl, see. I hate myself for it. Because I don't want the girl and still, I take it and—I love it! (p.19)

The power he has over women, combined with the knowledge that he has triumphed in some way over a superior increases his self-esteem. In his youth, Happy had always been much less successful than Biff:

he was the good brother who admired Biff; he carried his shoulder guards and enthused over the games in which Biff played. He has shared Willy's hopes for the future and to some extent shares Willy's dreams. He has his own dreams; to become rich, to be like Uncle Ben, to be able to 'retire Willy for life' (p.32), but reality catches up with him too: it is Willy who points out that he is too fond of women, of cars and of his apartment to do anything but carry on his life as it is. It is Happy's idea to sell sporting goods, to put on an exhibition in order to revive 'the old honour, and comradeship' (p.50). His dreams are centred on Biff, and, like the other dreams in the play centred on him, are dashed. Happy's main 'weakness' is his inability to resist women. A conquest gives him a feeling of power, and takes over from anything else. The scene in the restaurant is a good example of this. While waiting for Biff and his father, he decides to impress a girl in the restaurant with stories of his achievements and his work:

HAPPY: Why don't you bring her—excuse me, miss, do you mind? I sell champagne, and I'd like you to try my brand. Bring her a champagne, Stanley.

GIRL: That's awfully nice of you.

HAPPY: Don't mention it. It's all company money. (*He laughs.*)

GIRL: That's a charming product to be selling isn't it?

HAPPY: Oh, gets to be like everything else. Selling is selling, y'know.

GIRL: I suppose.

HAPPY: You don't happen to sell, do you?

GIRL: No, I don't sell.

HAPPY: Would you object to a compliment from a stranger. You ought to be on a magazine cover. (p.79-80)

He tells the girl that Biff is a great football player, and fortunately for the two of them, the girl knows little about the subject and so the pretence can continue. The incident may seem small on the surface, but it indicates a familiar trait in the Lomans: the need to pretend to be more than they actually are. Happy takes after Willy in this. Happy, however, has only contempt for the girl: when she leaves he says that she was 'on call' and that she is typical of the women around New York. Later, Linda describes them as 'whores'.

The extent of Happy's need to impress these girls may be judged from his comment later; Biff has revealed to Happy what happened in the interview and both realise Biff is the only one who can really help Willy. Happy's mind turns to other things, as he only thinks of getting away from the restaurant and taking the girls out:

HAPPY: (*starting after* BIFF): Where are you going?

MISS FORSYTHE: What's he so mad about?

HAPPY:	Come on girls, we'll catch up with him.
MISS FORSYTHE:	(*as* HAPPY *pushes her out*): Say, I don't like that temper of his!
HAPPY:	He's just a little overstrung, he'll be all right!
WILLY:	(*off left, as the* WOMAN *laughs*): Don't answer! Don't answer!
LETTA:	Don't you want to tell your father—
HAPPY:	No, that's not my father. He's just a guy. Come on, we'll catch Biff, and, Honey, we're going to paint this town! (p.91)

Everything must stop for Happy when he is faced with the possibility of enjoying himself with a woman, even to the extent of abandoning his father: denying all knowledge of him in fact. Happy never acquires Biff's ultimate self-knowledge and realisation of the truth; even after Willy's death, he still insists

> I'm staying right in this city, and I'm gonna beat this racket!... The Loman Brothers!... I'm gonna show you and everybody else that Willy Loman did not die in vain. He had a good dream. (p.111)

Typically, Happy has not learned the lesson of Willy's death, retaining the same beliefs and 'ideals' that he had before. He has not learned his true position—an 'assistant to the assistant'—and reality does not seem to have impressed itself upon him. He remains the Loman that he always was, incapable of interpreting the message of Willy's failure.

Linda

Linda tries to share in Willy's ideals, and suffers great torment as she observes Willy's decline, knowing that she is powerless to help. Her sharing can only go a small way, as she lacks the temperament to carry them out to the full. Miller sums her up at the beginning of the play:

> *Most often jovial, she has developed an iron repression of her exceptions to Willy's behaviour—she more than loves him, she admires him, as though his mercurial nature, his temper, his massive dreams and his little cruelties, served her only as sharp reminders of the turbulent longings within him, longings which she shares but lacks the temperament to utter and follow to their end.* (p.8)

Her admiration for Willy is, of course, part of her love for him, and is shown in several of the homely touches in her. She offers Willy support when he feels he has failed in his selling:

> LINDA: But you're doing wonderful, dear. You're making seventy to a hundred dollars a week.

WILLY: But I gotta be at it ten, twelve hours a day . . . I talk too
    much . . .
LINDA: You don't talk too much, you're just lively . . .

And she adds, when he seems to be depressed about his appearance,
that he is the 'handsomest' man in the world to her (pp.28–29). To her,
Willy is the best: a man who works and tries and has pride.

She is a simple person also, but that should not be taken in any
derogatory sense. Although failing to understand much of what has
happened to Willy, just as she fails to fathom what has occurred between him and Biff, she retains a belief in the need to treat human beings
properly:

LINDA: Then make Charley your father, Biff. You can't do that, can
    you? I don't say he's a great man. Willy Loman never made
    a lot of money. His name was never in the paper. He's not the
    finest character that ever lived. But he's a human being, and a
    terrible thing is happening to him. So attention must be paid.
    He's not to be allowed to fall into his grave like an old dog.
    Attention, attention must be finally paid to such a person.
    (p.44)

Her sons' treatment of Willy angers her; she places his welfare before
everything, sympathising and pretending for the sake of Willy's pride:

LINDA: . . . Now he takes his valises out of the car and puts them back
    and takes them out again and he's exhausted. Instead of
    walking he talks now. He drives seven hundred miles, and
    when he gets there no-one knows him any more, no-one
    welcomes him, and what goes through a man's mind, driving
    seven hundred miles home without earning a cent? Why
    shouldn't he talk to himself? Why? When he has to go to
    Charley and borrow fifty dollars a week and pretend to me
    that it's his pay? How long can that go on? How long? You
    see what I'm sitting here and waiting for? And you tell me he
    has no character? (p.45)

Her loyalty is a trait that cannot be over-emphasised; she encourages
and supports Willy, at the same time keeping a careful check on the
finances of the house, and at all times weighing the expenditure against
the income. This practical side of her is connected with her loyalty, as
she never pushes Willy into trying for more, knowing that he forces
himself to the limit anyway.

Her anger also stems from her beliefs in the Loman family, and the
memories she has of the happy times in the past. She sees the decline in
the relationship between Biff and Willy with sadness and again fails to

account for it: she asks Biff to explain why the two are so 'hateful' to each other (p.42).

This question could be answered by Biff, but he spares his mother's feelings. Earlier, her simplicity was mentioned. This can be seen in her attitude to her home in her reaction to characters who she regards as extreme. She wants to be satisfied in her present situation; for example, the exploits of Ben have no fascination for her:

LINDA: You're doing well enough, Willy!
BEN: (*to* LINDA): Enough for what, my dear?
LINDA: (*frightened of* BEN *and angry at him*): Don't say those things to him! Enough to be happy right here, right now. (*To* WILLY, *while* BEN *laughs*) Why must everybody conquer the world? You're well-liked and the boys love you, and some day—(*to* BEN)—why, old man Wagner told him just the other day that if he keeps it up he'll be a member of the firm, didn't he, Willy? (p.67)

This speech combines her fear of Ben, her belief in a happiness within the confines of her own situation, and her admiration for Willy. If this speech were to be considered alone, the conclusion might be that she prefers her present condition, but we also know that she shares Willy's ambitions: she dreams of a comfortable future without uncertainty.

There is, of course, uncertainty in Linda's way of life in the city, but one with which, given the poor economic circumstances of the Lomans, she feels she can deal. After his death, she repeats similar feelings to the ones quoted above:

LINDA: I can't understand it. At this time especially. First time in thirty-five years we were just about free and clear. He only needed a little salary. He was even finished with the dentist.
CHARLEY: No man only needs a little salary.
LINDA: I can't understand it. (p.110)

She has shared Willy's dreams to some extent, but she has not been able fully to understand his psychology, nor those of Biff and Happy. Willy wanted to be 'free' from all the restraints imposed by the city; she wants to be free from financial worries, but still sees herself as within the city; her last speech over Willy's grave emphasises this:

LINDA: . . . I don't understand it. Why did you ever do that? Help me, Willy, I can't cry. It seems to me that you're just on another trip. I keep expecting you, Willy, dear, and I can't cry . . . I made the last payment on the house today. Today, dear. And there'll be nobody home. (p.111–12)

She has tried to understand, but failed. Her last words are about the 'home': her mind focuses on her surroundings, and the need to make them as comfortable as possible. She is, in the end, a woman struggling to come to terms with the city, her husband and her sons.

Ben

'Uncle Ben' is, in Willy's words, 'a great man', an example for his sons to follow. He has been a ruthless businessman, rich, adventurous, not confined by any psychological restraints. Willy is impressed by him, emphasising to Biff and Happy that Ben is a Loman, that they can achieve what Ben has achieved:

> WILLY: . . . Listen to this. This is your Uncle Ben, a great man! Tell my boys, Ben!
> BEN: Why, boys, when I was seventeen I walked into the jungle, and when I was twenty-one I walked out . . . And by God I was rich.
> WILLY: (*to the boys*): You see what I been talking about? The greatest thing can happen!
> BEN: (*glancing at his watch*): I have an appointment in Ketchikan Tuesday week.
> WILLY: No, Ben! Please tell about Dad. I want my boys to hear. I want them to know the kind of stock they spring from.
> (p.37–38)

Willy sees Ben as a symbol for 'success', and when he advises Willy (p.66) to 'screw on your fists and you can fight for a fortune' he is describing his own business methods. 'Never fight fair', his advice to Biff, is also connected with this. He is contemptuous of Willy's way of life, assuming that anyone can become rich eventually—but he fails to realise that everyone does not have his personality or outlook on life. Linda's fear of him and of his attitude to life shows that she realises all men are not created the same. Ben is free to fight the way he does, and in the jungle of the business world he will come out on top.

Bernard

If Ben is the opposite of Willy, then Bernard is the opposite of Biff. While Biff was out being successful on the football field, Bernard was passing exams, and at the same time trying to encourage Biff to study more. He is dismissed by Willy as an 'anaemic', a boy never likely to grow into a successful man. Bernard, however, displays patience and dedication in his academic performances, rising eventually to become a top lawyer. Willy's outburst against Bernard, that he is a 'worm' (p.31) turns out to be ironic. Bernard becomes respected, rich and popular. By way of contrast, Willy meets Bernard after his success, and the contrast impresses itself upon Willy:

WILLY: *(after a pause)*: I'm—I'm overjoyed to see how you made the grade, Bernard, overjoyed. It's an encouraging thing to see a young man really—really—Looks very good for Biff—very—(*He breaks off, then*): Bernard—(*He is so full of emotion he breaks off again*)

BERNARD: What is it, Willy?

WILLY: *(small and alone)*: What—what's the secret?

BERNARD: What secret?

WILLY: How—how did you? Why didn't he ever catch on? (p.72)

Later, Charley reveals that Bernard is to argue a case in front of the Supreme Court. He has become one of the country's top lawyers; the contrast is quite explicit: Bernard has reached the top, achieving similar things to the ones which Willy wanted Biff to achieve.

Despite this, Bernard has lost none of his sympathy for the Loman family. Formerly, he wanted to help Biff with his math, to carry his headgear. . . . Now, he is prepared to sit down and talk to Willy about Biff, to try to understand Biff's change in attitude. Bernard, although sympathetic, is as powerless to help in the present as he was in the past: he can only sit and observe.

Charley

Charley, like Bernard, remains sympathetic towards the Lomans despite Willy's insults. Willy sees Charley as 'not a man' (p.34), a person similar to Bernard in his weakness, but someone whom he seems privately to admire. He admits to Linda that 'one thing about Charley. He's a man of few words, and they respect him.' Again, the contrast is established: Willy is not respected, nor, for that matter, is he a man of few words. Charley is amused by Willy's enthusiasm over a particular football game (p.70), yet sufficiently concerned about the well-being of the Lomans to lend money to Willy time after time. True, he hurts Willy's pride when he offers him a job, but this is out of genuine concern for Willy, as is his attempt to bring him down to earth, to face reality:

CHARLEY: Willy, when're you gonna realize that them things don't mean anything? You named him Howard, but you can't sell that. The only thing you got in this world is what you can sell, and the funny thing is that you're a salesman, and you don't know that. (p.76-77)

In the end, he remains as powerless as the others to help Willy; he may be Willy's 'best friend' but he can offer only a financial solution to Willy's problems: he can never solve Willy's inner problems.

Howard Wagner

Howard, Willy's employer, appears briefly in the play, and then only to tell Willy that he has lost his job. Willy suggests to him that he uses people as 'oranges', and that 'You can't eat the orange and throw the peel away—a man is not a piece of fruit' (p.64). Willy's judgement is extreme, and, although Howard does appear harsh on the surface, there seems little doubt that his words are accurate: 'If I had a spot I'd slam you right in but I just don't have a single solitary spot' (p.62).

Unwittingly, he unnerves Willy with his tape recorder, another possession that Willy cannot afford, a sign that he is insensitive to Willy's real position. He is obviously concerned for the firm, and feels it necessary to dismiss Willy despite his long service. He is a professional businessman—consideration for the firm must come first. He has no sentiment, which probably accounts for his success.

The Woman

She appears at intervals in the play, and her position in Willy's life becomes clearer as the action progresses. Willy was having an affair at the same time that Biff failed his math exam (when he was 17).

She is a woman out for a good time. She knows how to flatter Willy, how to keep him relying on her and, because of this, how to extract gifts from him. She promises Willy that she can send him 'right through to the buyers. No waiting at my desk any more'. She obviously knows Willy well enough to realise that this is the sort of promise that Willy needs, and such statements of his as 'I'm so lonely' are the sort of thing she needs to confirm her in her belief that she can keep Willy. She is a hard person, one for whom gentle persuasion means nothing. She cannot weigh up the situation on the entry of Biff and proves herself to be tactless and insensitive. All she can think of is her gift: 'You had two boxes of size nine sheers for me and I want them' she asserts. She is using Willy, exploiting his needs for her own ends. Significantly, she has no name—she is just an anonymous person.

The two girls

Letta and Miss Forsythe appear in the restaurant scene. They are easily impressed by the light chat of Happy and Biff, and ready to 'paint the town red' with them. Linda describes the two as 'whores': possibly true, but certainly they are two more girls out for a 'good time'.

Theatrical devices

Crucial scenes

(1) In Act Two, we finally learn the truth about Biff's rejection of the old ideals, and why he became antagonistic towards his father. Willy's 'fake' existence is also revealed. This is the scene that begins on page 91. Biff and Happy have been trying to impress the two girls in the restaurant, as they wish to take them out. This scene fades into a parallel one, as Willy's past affair with the Woman is revealed. He too has at one stage painted the town red, with a woman who has been as easy to acquire as the girls in the restaurant. It is almost a continuation of the Loman story, although Willy cannot see this. The flashback is part of the explanation of Willy's behaviour, and here the flashback is used to reveal Willy's conscience.

The affair that Willy had and Biff discovered has left a deep impression on the latter, and has altered the relationship between father and son. The scene is also a crucial one for the audience, explaining as it does Biff's troubles and why he has turned his back on the Loman way of life. We are shown Willy's infidelity, his need for support and his attitude towards Biff. Although the audience's suspicions have been aroused by earlier scenes (on page 30 for example), the affair is not confirmed until now. It has already been noticed how often Willy says he is 'lonely', despite the confident exterior. Here we find Willy repeating this statement, attempting to draw on the woman for support; yet the attempt is a sad one, for we realise that Willy is being used by this woman. Her words 'From now on, whenever you come to the office, I'll see that you go right through to the buyers. No waiting at my desk any more, Willy. You ruined me' (p.92) are not true, as her brashness shows. But he seems to want to accept all that she says. His reply to her is 'That's nice of you to say that'. She succeeds in supporting his self-esteem; she feeds him the words he wants to hear.

Yet this woman troubles his conscience; on the entry of Biff he attempts to hide her, or tries to make weak excuses. The jokes he has with Biff about the math teacher serve as a contrast—that is, the Willy/ Biff relationship before Biff discovers the truth. Biff at this stage still believes in his father and that he can persuade the math teacher to change the 'failed' grade. Now, his attitude changes completely after the shock of seeing the woman. Willy cannot cover up by lying. Biff's attitude changes in fact to his 'present day' one. The idea behind the words 'you liar . . . you fake! You phony little fake!' (p.95) is repeated at the climax of the play.

(2) The climax of the play arrives when Biff finally decides to leave the

house, and is forced to confront the family with his views of what the Loman family is and the sort of existence that they lead. Tired of the pretence that they have been living, he wants first of all to leave quietly, feeling that the family—and Willy in particular—can brighten up once he has left. This is a misjudgement, obviously, because Willy still lives for Biff's success. Willy's anger at his decision to leave provokes the by now familiar response that he is a 'phony' (p.103), and from that point in the play Biff's response to the Loman ideals pours out. 'We never told the truth for ten minutes in this house', is a comment with which we cannot argue: we have heard about Willy's ideals so often, and we have seen the reality of the household situation; we have also observed his attitude towards the 'great' Biff, and we have had to contrast this with what Biff is really like. What we are now hearing from Biff is a comment on Willy's enormous capacity for self-deception. Biff is also attempting to bring Willy face to face with reality, to point out markedly that he is tired of the 'hot air' of the Lomans, of the false pride, of the refusal to admit that 'I'm a dime a dozen, and so are you!' (p.105). The door of his life is not 'wide open' as Willy insists it is; Biff has had to face that in Oliver's office, hating the idea of being deprived of the 'open air'. He has to be what he really is, even if this means facing up to the fact that he can't earn 'one dollar an hour'. Reality does not obscure his affection for Willy—while recognising his falsity, he is also moved to tears, because he is 'broken' by his outburst. Perhaps 'affection' is too strong a word: he is confused by Willy and disturbed by his failure to communicate his views to him. He realises the truth, but he cannot make Willy agree with him.

Why is this the 'climax' of the play? After this scene, the action is almost complete—the break between the two is at last made apparent; any hope there might have been for the relationship is finally crushed, even for Willy. Unconsciously, he knows the end has been reached. 'Climax' is the right word—the scene shows an explosion of emotion and brings into the open a situation that can never be improved upon or reversed. The action of the play has built up to this: there might have been hope, if Biff could have kept up the pretence, or if Willy could have kept his sanity, but none of these happen. Willy's death becomes inevitable in his mind after this scene, because life becomes meaningless to him now that he can offer nothing to Biff.

Lighting and music

Miller uses the theatrical devices of lighting and the music effectively in this play. If the Stage Directions are followed carefully, these two properties become symbolic. The opening stage direction is a good example of this, expressing as it does a mood: *'A melody is heard, played upon a flute. It is small and fine, telling of grass and trees and the horizon.'* (p.7)

The flute here is an 'expressionist' device. It means something other than a tune, a representation of life in the open, a life full of hope and peace. By way of contrast, Miller states that the apartments are surrounded by 'an angry glow of orange' (p.7). This colour represents the anger of people who fall in the city, who are deprived of promise, who, like Biff, are angered by the way of life.

The flute is introduced once more (p.13) as Willy begins to imagine a happier life in the past. The flute is particularly suited to this, as it is an instrument which can be easily-associated with nostalgia.

At the beginning of Act Two, hope seems to have arisen once more: Biff is going to the interview with Oliver, there is promise that the Lomans can live together as a family unit. Miller represents to us the happiness of Willy in the dialogue, and introduces the new act with 'gay and bright' music. The mood on the stage is established by a fairly simple but effective device; and the audience is attuned to the mood of the characters on stage.

Miller insists that the character of the Woman should not be mistaken and he supplies a stage direction (p.91) that *'raw, sensuous music'* should accompany their speech. The relationship between the two has been raw and sensuous although Willy may be blind to this. The music also reveals another side to Willy, since he too is associated with the music. It is a side unknown to Biff, a side which may surprise us but which we should recognise as a vital part of the play, since it establishes the 'phony' side of Willy.

Symbolic characters

Although none of the characters in the play is completely symbolic, Willy interprets two of them as virtually symbolic characters. For instance, he sees Biff as a god, a man great enough to supersede anyone that has gone before him:

> WILLY: Like a young god. Hercules—something like that. And the sun, the sun all around him. Remember how he waved to me? Right up from the field, with the representatives of three colleges standing by? And the buyers I brought, and the cheers when he came out—Loman, Loman, Loman! God Almighty, he'll be great yet. A star like that, magnificent, can never really fade away! (p.54)

His hopes have been raised once more, and he goes to bed dreaming of the new possibilities. He says 'Look at the moon moving between the buildings' (p.54). The images he uses in connection with Biff and with the future are ones of light: at this stage, the Lomans seem to be emerging into the 'light', with Biff as the main hope. The images here are connected with the earlier images of the garden and the open air, both associated with lightness and happiness by Willy and Biff. Willy however, is trapped in the 'concrete jungle' where

> the grass don't grow any more, you can't raise a carrot in the backyard. They should've had a law against apartment houses. Remember those two beautiful trees out there? (p.12)

The man who has escaped the jungle and has found his fortune is Ben, apparently the opportunist of the family.

Ben, however, is a more elusive character in terms of Willy's 'symbolism'. He represents all that Willy wishes the boys to be, yet his actions in the past are not firmly established. Willy *imagines* him all the time, and he may well exaggerate his memories. This is what makes Ben elusive; he is, for Willy, a symbol of all that is 'good in the land of opportunity'.

The last point about Ben can be linked very closely to the stage directions. In them Miller states that a director should make it clear to the audience whenever Willy is stepping beyond the bounds of reality:

> *Before the house lies an apron, curving beyond the forestage into the orchestra. This forward area serves as the back yard as well as the locale of all Willy's imaginings and of his city scenes. Whenever the action is in the present the actors observe the imaginary wall lines, entering the house only through its door at the left. But in scenes of the past these boundaries are broken, and characters enter or leave a room by stepping 'through' a wall onto the forestage.* (p.7)

Willy's imagination breaks the bounds of present time, so the physical properties on the stage must represent this: the action (in the characters' minds) and the set correspond to and complement each other.

Themes

The great country

One of Willy's basic beliefs is in the 'land of opportunity', a land where men were created equal, with equal opportunity to become rich and successful. America is this land. Despite his standard of living, despite the obvious fact that he has not 'made good' in American society, he never criticises that society for long: it remains a place in which a young ambitious person can succeed.

Biff has not found himself because he is a 'lazy bum' in 'the greatest country in the world' (p.11). From hard work will come success, as though the land rewarded harder work with riches. Now, this may well be true in certain contexts, but here Miller is trying to show how such simplistic notions can break down: in other words, they are not *absolute* in value. There is no universal law which guarantees success. The other quality that Willy believes in is also linked with this: 'personality' is necessary for success. Biff has 'personal attractiveness' (p.11), can work hard (at least, according to Willy), and so must succeed. What Willy fails to take into account is the *individual* and his own hopes, fears and ambitions. Biff is simply not *like* Ben, and, although Willy listens to Ben, he does not understand his advice. Ben recognises that the city is a 'jungle' and there is one way to escape from it and achieve the wealth that brings admiration. His advice to Biff is 'never fight fair with a stranger' (p.38), advice that he has put into practice and which has made him successful. But Biff cannot follow this. He is not a person of Ben's kind, he is incapable of surviving on his own. Biff depended heavily on his father as a youth, and on the 'break' with him he became lost. The theory of the 'land of opportunity', then, diminishes considerably in the light of personal experience and personal endeavours and toughness.

America, however, is also the land of the great outdoors. Several times in the play Willy mentions the possibility of the good life in the country; for example (p.22), he visualises swinging on a hammock between two elm trees, and hates the new order that has insisted on the two elms being cut down, while Biff also finally sees the country as a satisfying place to live. But outdoor life is not lucrative. There is a paradox here: America *is* the land of opportunity in the sense that a man is allowed to choose the way in which he will live. Biff has been pressured away from the sort of life he wishes to lead, but the life is still there. The pressure is to join the middle classes and earn money.

Middle classes and money

During the time the play was written the middle classes had suffered a decline. The real value of their money had dwindled; they were struggling to make enough money to maintain their former standard of living. Now, Willy seems to be a typical case as he too feels these financial pressures, feels obliged to keep up the pretence of a successful bourgeois existence. We know from his early conversations with Linda that Willy is continually in financial difficulties: he borrows from Charley to pay his life assurance, pretending to Linda that he has earned it from the job. When Howard Wagner shows Willy his new tape recorder, he is impressed and asserts 'I'm definitely going to get one', because they are only 'a hundred and a half' (p.61). We know very well that Willy cannot possibly afford one, but he has to keep up the pretence of being able to acquire material goods. Willy has declined, but cannot face up to this in public. He presents a facade because the sort of things he wants are those which the successful businessman is supposed to possess. Again the pressure is to be 'successful' and success can be measured in material goods, at least in the society that Miller is presenting to us. Riches and success are inseparable for Willy. This is one of the reasons why he cannot understand Biff, who seems to have no interest in making money. Willy does not see that there may be other values, ones which, although not financially beneficial, are more suited to the individuals concerned. Biff sees that the Lomans belong somewhere else, a society in which they can be 'carpenters', in the open air. Willy insists on keeping up appearances and refusing to face reality.

The 'fake' life and reality

Willy wants to see himself as a successful businessman, a man for whom everyone will have respect, and, because of this, when he dies he will have a grand funeral. He wants and even anticipates a funeral like Dave Singleman's, a man who had 'hundreds of salesman and buyers at his funeral' (p.63). That was the 'real' death of a salesman for Willy. But those days are now gone, and a different set of values are apparent. The reality is, as Willy admits, that 'they seem to laugh at me' (p.28). The old need to have personality which made for success in the world of business seems to have disappeared. Reality is in the apartment block, the debts and Willy's constant refusal to recognise city life for what it is.

Biff tells Willy that he is a fake, never speaking the 'truth'. He means that the Lomans are 'out of place' in city life, but his basic aim is to try to shock Willy into some self-knowledge. Willy is not aware of the falsity of his existence; as Biff says (p.104) 'you blew me so full of hot air I never could stand taking orders from anybody!' Biff has been deceived by Willy into assuming a grander status than he actually deserves. He has filled him with pride, making it all the more difficult for Biff to realise that 'I'm a dime a dozen and so are you!' Even after Biff's outburst, Willy still fails to understand. 'Why is he crying?' he asks Linda. All Biff can do is to reply: 'Will you take that phony dream and burn it before something happens?' To which Willy replies 'isn't that remarkable? Biff—he likes me!' (p.106). Willy still lives in a world revolving around Biff, a world of success, a world that the Lomans simply do not inhabit. Willy has insisted on carrying out his fake existence to the end. This trait is continued to some extent in Happy, who believes that he 'will show everybody that Willy Loman did not die in vain' (p.111). We know that Happy cannot do this—he will never be a great businessman either. Willy dies 'not knowing who he was', still believing in one dream of success in the great land.

Biff's view of Willy as a fake stems of course from the shock he received on finding out about Willy's affair with the woman. This was the first time he used the word 'fake', and it appears to have been on his mind ever since. Now the context of this belief changes: Biff comes to regard the whole of the Loman way of life as false. It is as though this one event has made Biff realise that the Loman family, under the influence of Willy, has been living under false pretences. He looks around and sees the ordinariness of their existence, their mundane jobs and the impossibility that they could ever rise above what they are. Biff's reaction is extreme—he abandons his school career, his games and indeed any ambition he had formerly. He has been pushed into this psychologically in order to try to find where the real Lomans belong, insisting that he avoids the false existence and abandoning all associations with his past life.

Inter-connection of themes

The themes and characterisation in the play are inseparable: Miller creates in Willy a typical member of the middle class with middle-class ambitions, while at the same time he is a psychological study: self-deluding, a man unable to come to terms with reality. Biff is also a study, and he is also part of the whole 'theme' of the fake existence of the Lomans: it is what *defines* much of his character. But no one character represents one idea on its own—the characters embody several, in the depths of their personalities. 'Themes', 'ideas' and 'characters' are all part of the whole work of art, and the inter-connection must be realised and brought out. The over-simplified 'categorising' of a literary work cannot occur here: the work's various components are interlocked.

Critical problems

The play is meant to be a modern tragedy, and is linked to Miller's essay on *Tragedy and the Common Man*. In this essay, Miller tries to redefine our notion of tragedy. Previously, the tragic hero (in Shakespeare for example) had been a man who was somehow placed above ordinary mortals, who, either through his depth of suffering or his nobility of nature felt and suffered more than we could be expected to do in everyday life. The hero also suffers death at the end, his downfall being a result of a fatal flaw in his character, a trait which he cannot help as it is a part of his makeup, but which causes the tragedy and eventually his death. Sympathy plays a significant part in the action: the audience must feel that the man has suffered beyond what could be expected, and has paid beyond measure for whatever mistake he made, a result of a 'flaw'.

Willy, however, does not fit into this traditional pattern—he is an 'average man'. Indeed, Miller's point is that Willy *must* be average: he tries to rise above this, but fails. Nor does he appear to have one 'fatal flaw': he is proud, but also false; he loves his family almost too much, yet has affairs. Miller was aware of some of the discrepancies between his 'hero' and the traditional tragic hero, and attempted a new definition of what tragedy means to the twentieth-century man.

In his essay, Miller makes several strong statements. Firstly, he attempts to define tragic feeling and what produces it in an audience: 'tragic feeling is evoked in us', he writes, 'when we are in the presence of a character who is ready to lay down his life, if need be, to secure one thing—his sense of personal dignity.' This statement seems so obviously to have been written with Willy in mind that it is difficult not to come to the conclusion that Miller deliberately wrote it to answer any possible objections that might be raised about the nature of the tragedy in *Death of a Salesman*. If Miller is right, then Willy's fate *is* tragic: but where does that leave other tragedies, particularly in the light of the comment, in the same essay, that tragedy is 'the heart and spirit of the average man'? Do we say that there is room in criticism for *two* forms of tragedy, one more or less exclusive to the twentieth century?

Perhaps a truer picture may be seen on a closer examination of Miller's motives behind the essay, for in it he not only attempts a redefinition of tragedy but also indicates his *social* concerns:

> The tragic right is a condition of life, a condition in which the human personality is able to flower and realize itself. The wrong is the condition which suppresses man, perverts the flowing out of his love and creative instinct . . . tragedy . . . points the heroic finger at the enemy of man's freedom. The thrust for freedom is the quality in tragedy which exalts.

Miller's concern is for degrees of social freedom, and sympathy results when a man, struggling against social pressures, is pushed further back, achieving little in his struggle for freedom, and having degrees of freedom removed from him. Willy fits very closely in with these ideas; he is a man trapped by a conventional notion of what is 'right': the successful man, the man of personality, is defined by his wealth and *must*, by some process in the 'great country', be popular and known. Yet the city rejects this idea, for it is an image of the older form of America, before the city took over. Willy is a product of certain social and economic pressures outside himself, which he misjudges, and by which he is destroyed. He cannot fit into the definition of 'successful' that society has imposed, so in those terms he is a failure. He does not have an ability to battle against these pressures, and is finally destroyed by his commitment to them.

The play can be seen to have several weaknesses, however, despite all Miller's attempts to alter our view of the tragic hero. In Shakespearian tragedy the death of the hero contained some meaning: lessons were learned and the remaining characters gained knowledge and experience from the witnessing of the events. We feel also that society will gain from the deaths and that the suffering has not been in vain.

It appears that Miller believes that if society were changed, needless deaths, such as Willy's, could be avoided. Willy is a man struggling to gain his 'rightful position in society', and his suicide must lead to the question: 'how can this be prevented and how is it possible to change society for the betterment of all?'

This question is not answered. Willy is all the time attempting to become a part of this society, but it rejects him. He actively attempts to make himself liked and accepted, but society merely seems to mock. There is no chance of heroism or change in Miller's portrait of twentieth-century society: however much man may struggle, he is faced with impossible odds. Willy's struggle is sterile: we *know* Biff will not become great, nor Happy as rich as he imagines. Beyond the immediate family, little attention is paid to Willy's death. Willy's lies have been for nothing, too, since the main recipient of all of them—Biff—realises the truth. Willy's hope will not outlast Willy, and will never see the light of day.

This may be too harsh. Perhaps sympathy should not be limited to a conventional view of the tragic hero. Willy lives closer to our experience than many protagonists, he is struggling with the pressures of twentieth-century life: of money, of the city, of the family, of the job, while his weaknesses are those which ordinary humans share. Loneliness, the inability to decide exactly what one wants, the breakdown of communications between the two generations, are all part of our lives to some extent. Miller shows that man is isolated, and, even though he struggles, he may be faced with impossible odds. Linda's attitude may be a final summary—that people should be treated like human beings and not allowed to go to waste 'like old dogs'.

Part 4

Hints for study

Detailed study

A useful starting point for any detailed study of the text is to make a list of the main themes which occur, noting how each one is related to the others and cannot be isolated from them. Such a list might read:

(*a*) twentieth-century middle-class life
(*b*) the decline of the middle classes
(*c*) 'appearance' and 'reality'
(*d*) the pressure to lead a 'fake' existence
(*e*) success
(*f*) the American myth of the 'great country'
(*g*) the desire for freedom
(*h*) the importance of personality

Note that these overlap: the pressure on the middle classes was to be successful in the great land of opportunity, since all are free to pursue success. Yet, when a character like Willy feels himself under pressure, and cannot respond to it, he has to pretend to himself and to others, to assume the appearance of success, while hiding himself from reality. It is the same with Biff: he has been placed under pressure by Willy, but has come to realise he cannot live up to his demands, while he also comes to see that his family lead a false existence.

Remember that the themes and the characters cannot be separated from each other. A theme is not an abstract idea divorced from the minds of the people in the play. How this works may be judged from a close reading of certain crucial scenes. If you reconsider one of the flashback scenes in Act One (the scene on pages 37–41) you will realise that, at this stage in the play, Willy is recalling scenes from the past. He has hopes for the future success of Happy and Biff, believes in the possibility of greatness for them. Willy sees Ben as an example of achievement, a man of adventure and fortune. Ben is rich—and so has achieved Willy's dream of money, yet Willy can never copy him and 'never fight fair': his ideal is to be 'well-liked'. Ben recognises and points out that his father 'made more in a week than a man like you could make in a lifetime', which is the reality of the situation that Willy cannot face: we know this to be true from earlier scenes, in which Linda and Willy have been shown struggling to make ends meet.

Ben's achievement is that he walked out of the city 'jungle' and became rich through personal enterprise and ruthlessness. Here, then, the characters express many of the themes in the play: money, success in life, the realities of a particular situation, the need for freedom and its availability. Look at some other scenes in the same way. On pages 46-8 for example, Biff begins to express his doubts about the Lomans and the fact that they might not 'belong'; in Act Two (pp.60-4) Willy's failures and his self-deception are brought out, while the restaurant scene later (pp.86-90) indicates the breakdown in communications between Biff and Willy, and ultimately leads to Biff's rejection of the fake life. The flashback scene to the hotel, and Biff's discovery of Willy's affair is another crucial scene, while the climax of the play (pp.102-6) shows the final break and leads to the death of Willy.

Quotations

Because the various themes overlap and the characters express those themes, it is clear that any essay dealing with themes must also deal with characters: so an analysis of themes should contain discussion of the characters. In order to make a point properly, it should be supported by relevant quotations from the text. Quotations show knowledge of the play, indicate the reader's ability to grapple with the play's problems and reveal how much insight the reader has had into the play. A good way of using quotations is to make a point about the play, quote a speech or part of a dialogue and analyse the precise points that the quotations bring out. For example, if you were arguing that Willy is a person who lives for the past, that he dreams of success for himself and Biff without being aware of reality, you might quote the following speech and argue from it:

> WILLY: Like a young god. Hercules—something like that. And the sun, the sun all around him. Remember how he waved to me? Right up from the field, with the representatives of three colleges standing by? And the buyers I brought, and the cheers when he came out—Loman, Loman, Loman! God Almighty, he'll be great yet. A star like that, magnificent, can never really fade away. (p.54)

This passage is typical of Willy's indulgence in the past and the former glories of Biff, successful at sport in his school days. Willy assumes that he will be successful now in business, but he is to be sadly disappointed: we know of Biff's doubts from some of his earlier speeches. Willy's language is also significant, as he sees Biff as a 'god' and a 'star': Willy has not faced up to the reality that Biff may well fail, charged as he is with enthusiasm at the thought of Biff gaining employment with Bill

Oliver. Business is his life, and he assumes that it must be Biff's: not until Biff's failure does Willy have to confront reality.

An example of how the play reaches its climax is Biff's speech in Act Two, pages 104–5. Biff, finally deciding that he is not part of city life, brings home the message to Willy:

> I stopped in the middle of that office building and I saw—the sky. I saw the things that I love in this world. The work and the food and the time to sit and smoke. And I looked at the pen and said to myself, what the hell am I grabbing this for? Why am I trying to become what I don't want to be? What am I doing in an office, making a contemptuous, begging fool of myself, when all I want is out there, waiting for me the minute I say I know who I am! (p.105)

He rejects city life, preferring the 'time' available in the country. He has been 'lost' so far, struggling under Willy's pressure, but now knows what he wants and he can also see the Lomans for what they are. This is the climax of the play and the turning point for Willy: everything is in the open, and there is only one way in which Willy can help Biff: by committing suicide.

Arrangement of material

Essays should be orderly in argument and arrangement: use one paragraph to express one idea or theme, another to analyse a particular character, bringing out the relationship between the two. Essays should *develop* an argument: they should build up to a complete picture of the topic under consideration. A useful way of building up an argument is to ask yourself a series of questions which relate to the appearance of the characters and the themes. For example:

(1) When does the character first appear?
(2) What is his/her function in the play?
(3) How does what he/she says at first compare or contrast with some of his/her later statements?
(4) Why does the character say what he/she does?
(5) Are we to take what the character says at face value, or should we question his/her motives?
(6) Is the author attempting to build up sympathy for the character? If so, why?
(7) Is there any theme introduced by the character, and how is it developed?
(8) Has the character/theme changed by the end of the play?
(9) What point is the author trying to make about the character/theme?

Questions

It is impossible to anticipate what questions might be raised about a particular text but the ones below are typical of the sort of essays which you might be expected to write. Remember also that although the wording of questions will be different from those below, the *meaning* may well be the same. If the topic appears difficult, ask yourself precisely what the question seems to be driving at, and to which characters you will have to give most attention. Plot summary should be avoided in an essay question unless specifically asked for, which is on rare occasions. Examiners are interested in your ability to analyse rather than memorise.

(1) Discuss the nature of the relationship between Willy and Biff.
(2) 'Willy's reliance on "personality" is misguided and out-of-date'. Discuss.
(3) Is Willy Loman a tragic hero?
(4) Miller defined his aim in writing the play as being 'to set forth what happens when a man does not have a grip on the forces of life.' Do you see Willy as this kind of man?
(5) 'Biff's rejection of Willy's ideals is the climax of his self-discovery.' Discuss.
(6) What is the importance of the flashback scenes in the play?
(7) 'Willy's image of America is a mistaken one: it is no longer the land of opportunity but a concrete jungle.' Discuss.
(8) What is the function of sound and music in the play?
(9) 'Willy's lies reflect the vain hope he has. He is a state of perpetual optimism about everything.' Discuss.
(10) What are the functions of Linda and Happy in the play?
(11) 'Willy's death shows that the American dream is a phoney dream.' Discuss.

Answers

Answers to questions (2) and (5) might be on the lines of the following:

(2) 'Willy's reliance on 'personality' is misguided and out-of-date'. Discuss.

Willy is an old-fashioned salesman, believing that the power of personality, the ability to make oneself liked anywhere, is a sufficient quality to ensure sales and success. Several times during the play he mentions he is 'liked' and, during the flashback scenes particularly, says that Biff will also be liked and therefore successful. Despite the financial troubles, or maybe even because of them, he still relies on his personality as the basis of his ability as a salesman—he says to Linda 'I'll knock'em dead next week. I'll go to Hartford. I'm very well liked in Hartford.' Yet we see that his philosophy just doesn't work any more: the reminders from Linda of the domestic difficulties indicate this to the audience. Willy's ideas of 'the salesman' stem from what he has heard of 'Dave Single-man'. In his speech (p.64) he makes it clear that he regards Singleman as *the* salesman—popular, and using his popularity to succeed in his trade. He misjudges his own potential: he has not the personality that can attract large sales.

He also misjudges the times. He fails to realise that the days of Singleman have gone, and that the successful businessman is a man like Ben: ruthless, caring little for the feelings of others, never fighting fair. America is no longer the country of leisure—where the 'velvet slippers' can be easily gained, but a land of ruthless opportunism, need-ing hard-headed, emotionless adventure as a formula for success. Willy misjudges this, and suffers for it, living as he does in the past. He cannot adapt successfully to life in the new America.

---

(5) 'Biff's rejection of Willy's ideals is the climax of his self-discovery.' Discuss.

At the beginning of the play, Biff is introduced to us a confused man, who is attempting to 'find himself': Linda describes him as 'lost'. This is, in a sense, true, and one aspect of the play deals with Biff's discovery of what he wants from life. He has been a drifter, avoiding contact with the family as far as possible, since he realises—only vaguely at first—that communication between himself and Willy is impossible. 'I can't get near him', he says (p.15).

He also seems to be confused about what kind of life he should pursue, feeling the need to be out of doors, yet aware that this is not a way of gaining a lot of money.

He is torn between a life in the city and one in the country. This contrasts with the speech he makes at the climax of the play (see p.105). By this stage in the play he has become aware that he cannot fit in with the pressures of middle-class life. He prefers time to sit in the open, and more leisure. There is no ambiguity in the later speech, none of the dilemma that appeared in the early parts of the play.

Biff experiences much in the course of the play to bring him to this conclusion. His report on the events in Bill Oliver's office (p.84), makes it clear that he has realised that a life of success in the city must remain a dream—but Willy's dream, not his. He determines on leaving that life for good. The life of the city, with its apparent attractions of success and money, is not for him. He discovers he cannot lead a false existence, one which he believes Willy has led. This means he has to leave behind the ideals—and the Lomans.

Part 5
Suggestions for further reading

The text

The most accessible edition of *Death of a Salesman* and the one used throughout this study is that published by Penguin Books, Harmondsworth, 1961

Other works by Arthur Miller

Collected Plays, Viking Press, New York, 1957

General reading

BROWN, J.R: and HARRIS, BERNARD (EDS.): *American Theatre,* Stratford-Upon-Avon Studies Number 10, Edward Arnold, London, 1967. This contains an essay by Eric Mottram entitled 'Arthur Miller: the development of a Political Dramatist in America', (pp.127–62)

FRENZ, HORST (ED.): *American Playwrights on Drama*, Hill and Wang, New York, 1965. Contains Miller's essay 'Tragedy and the Common Man', (pp.79–83)

HAYMAN, RONALD: *Arthur Miller*, Heinemann, London, 1970

PORTER, THOMAS E.: *Myth and Modern American Drama*, Wayne State University Press, Detroit, 1969. Consult especially pp.127–152

WEALES, GERALD: *American Drama since World War II*, Harcourt, New York, 1962

WELLAND, D.S.R.: *Arthur Miller* (Writers and Critics Series), Oliver and Boyd, Edinburgh and London, 1961

WELLAND, DENNIS: *Miller, A Study of his Plays*, Eyre and Methuen, London, 1979

The author of these notes

BRIAN W. LAST is a graduate of the Universities of Leeds and Stirling. He has been a Lecturer in English at Ahmadu Bello University, Nigeria, and at King Alfred's College, Winchester, and, until 1985, was Senior Lecturer at Mohammed V University, Rabat. Dr. Last now teaches part-time. He has written articles on the poetry of Keats and Soyinka and a study of eighteenth-century fiction.